SIMPLY AMAZING WOMEN

by the author of

Simply Amazing Special Authors Edition

K . C . A R M S T R O N G

WMAP Publishing
24 Oakland Ave.
Port Jefferson, NY
www.wmapradio.com

WMAP reports recollections gleaned through its interviews and does not maintain the legitimacy in portrayals of any action or person. We believe in our interviewees to be accurate, truthful and honestly represent the facts as they recall and understand them. Each interview has been reviewed by the person interviewed who assumes all responsibility for accurate portrayal of events and actions by themselves and others and does not necessarily represent the views of WMAP Radio or its associates.

Cover Designer: Klassic Designs working at 99designs
Cover Photographer: Erin Holst
Interior Designer: charlyn_designs
Editor: Virginia Bartol

Library of Congress Control Number: 2020905742

ISBN: 978-1-7347058-0-5 (Hardcover Edition)
ISBN: 978-1-7347058-2-9 (Paperback Edition)
ISBN: 978-1-7347058-1-2 (eBook Edition)

Printed in the United States of America

WMAP Publishing
24 Oakland Ave.
Port Jefferson, NY
www.wmapradio.com
(631) 909-8400

DEDICATION

I wish to dedicate this book to three amazing women I work with. Kellie Koch and Capriana McMurray are two of the best interviewers I have ever had the privilege to watch grow and excel at WMAP Radio. They have done amazing interviews and have even written questions for the incredible stories you are about to read. They are two kind, talented, hard working professionals, and I'd put their skills up against the best in the business. I get the credit, so I'd like to dedicate this book to them. They are enthusiastic, positive, love making a difference and always have smiles on their faces. Kelly and Capriana are not only incredible at their jobs, but they are both women of character, and I probably don't tell them how much I appreciate them as much as I should. But I am telling them and all of you now. Thank you, Kellie and Cap. I'd also like to thank my station manager, Autumn Maglia, for her outstanding creativity and ability to keep me on task. I don't know what I'd do without her organization!

If you know anything about me, you know the most important person in my life is my best friend, my inspiration, my idol—and I call her Mom. If my life ends today, nothing compares to the times, lessons and memories that I have with the luckiest part of my life. I believe in people, and in anything for that matter, only because of one amazing lady. You are so smart, strong, thoughtful and always know what to do. These memories we create mean more to me than anything in this world. If there is anything good about me, it is because of you.

CONTENTS

PREFACE

I'm writing this preface in the midst of a global pandemic-coronavirus (COVID-19).

This is a first for all of us, and we're each choosing our own response—fear, panic, stockpiling goods we may or may not need, and also spending time with our families, helping and sharing with our neighbors, calling friends we haven't checked in with for a while.

Now that I'm getting older, and knowing that nobody is guaranteed tomorrow, I find a lesson or realization in everything. Every story in this book, just like yours and mine, includes what seems to be a personal pandemic that one has to somehow get through.

WMAP's *Simply Amazing* series began before this new world-wide emergency, but the need for positive examples is always with us. I hope that by the time you read this, the current crisis will be past, but I know heartache and severe challenges are always present.

I've been told that *Simply Amazing Special Author's Edition* has raised people from disappointment and despair to new beginnings. I hope *Simply Amazing Women* will likewise uplift you and remind you of the strength of the individual. We can meet this new challenge and each one that comes our way. Be inspired by these Amazing Women and what their best qualities say about all of us.

K. C. Armstrong
Port Jefferson, N.Y.
May 2020

INTRODUCTION

Simply Amazing Women celebrates our mothers, sisters, wives and daughters who rise above unspeakable adversity to help ease the path of others. Women bring us into the world and teach us to love, nurture and protect.

People think I am prone to nonsense, but I want to be serious for a few minutes and tell you about a perfect example of toughness, determination and depth of pain threshold that I saw on TV last weekend. I was watching Joanna Jedrzejczyk and Weili Zhang fight for the Championship of the UFC at 115 pounds. Though I was watching this by myself, I actually stood up and cheered for both of these amazing women. I wasn't hoping for anyone to get hurt or to get punched; I was cheering because I was so inspired by the tenacity and focus that these two women displayed. They never quit. They went five full rounds with an incredible mental toughness and obvious passion for their sport and for winning. Although injured, they kept fighting with all their hearts. Even if you don't like MMA, you would still have been impressed with the passionate devotion of these two.

Every chapter in this book will show you a fight of the same intensity. The women you'll read about may not be throwing literal punches, but they are fighting their own battles toward self-improvement, healing, and helping others.

Even if our personal battle is not in the ring, our problems can overwhelm us. When our lives are turned upside down, it's common to feel betrayal, confusion, and even outrage. How we handle those emotions—by turning our trauma inward, outward, or by blocking the pain all together—is an individual matter. But releasing that pain, facing it, fighting back, and finding healing is a huge undertaking. Like Joanna and Weili, the women in this book have fought back with unbelievable courage, and we can applaud and learn from each of them.

Each punch I witnessed in that Championship fight reminded me of the abuse the characters in these chapters have taken. Whether the punches were physical, mental, or emotional, each woman you will read about here stood tall, stared down her opponent, and left the ring a true champ.

If I know anything at all, I know that women are tougher and definitely more resilient than men. The women in this book have courageously made public the details of their experiences and laid out for you a path that worked for them to recover. The exact same method of healing may not be yours, but you have a range of possibilities that demonstrate that we all—men and women—are capable of taking charge of our minds, bodies, and emotions.

The answer may be forgiveness, acceptance, enhancing your faith, or something else—but these brave women will show you what worked for them. I hope you will think about their journeys and adapt whatever will help you with yours.

FORGIVENESS

an interview with Kathy Bidelman

*Kathy's religious faith and her parents' example
taught her the healing power of forgiveness.*

INTRODUCTION:

Kathy Bidelman's story seems like it can't be real. I don't mean to personalize every chapter, but get used to it; I'm doing it! (lol). This chapter starts with what may first read as fiction, but—believe me—the story is all too real to Kathy and her family. If you are like me, you do your best to live by the *Golden Rule*: you know, "Do unto others as you would have others do unto you." I think most of the time I do an OK job, but I won't lie to you. When I'm deceived, wronged, or disrespected, I am no Kathy Bidelman. I suspect you may not be, either. One of the hardest things to do is hang on to the faith that things will work themselves out, even when we don't know how, why, or when. Kathy showed me that the person who hurts the most is the person who clings to anger or revenge. I challenge you to read her example and remember it the next time you want to get even.

Kathy is one of the kindest people I know. She's a good Christian and the daughter of a preacher and his wonderful wife. The strength of the family's religious beliefs and the compassion of their Church community were a great help during the tragic accident that turned their worlds upside down. Kathy learned a valuable lesson which she generously shares with all of us: forgiveness is not a random feeling that arises spontaneously when you are wronged. It is a conscious decision, made with love and mercy and is as much a gift to the victim as to the perpetrator of an unspeakable act. Thank you, Kathy, for sharing with us this hard-earned wisdom.

INTERVIEW:

K. C. Armstrong: Our next guest is Kathy Bidelman. She is kind and compassionate, but the greatest thing I have learned from her is the healing power of forgiveness. Kathy, welcome to the show.

Kathy Bidelman: Thank you K. C. How are you? Thanks for having me on.

K. C. Armstrong: Well, I'm so psyched that you're here! You've knocked people out over here at the station because everybody thinks my friends are so nice now that they've met you. (Smiles)

Kathy Bidelman: Well you do have a lot of nice friends! Look at the first book you wrote, *Simply Amazing Special Author's Edition*—all those incredible people!

K. C. Armstrong: Thanks, Kathy. You are in good company for sure. So let's first get a little background about your early life, OK? You were born and raised in Pennsylvania, the daughter of a pastor. Hey, no pressure, right?

Kathy Bidelman: Right, K.C. I'm from Johnstown, a coal mining town an hour and a half east of Pittsburgh. Johnstown is known as "the flood city" because we've experienced three devastating floods since 1889, and we feel like we're

I knew my eternity is set because my home is in Heaven

pretty much due for another big one. We sure get a lot of rain.

K. C. Armstrong: And your father was a preacher. What was it like to be a preacher's kid?

Kathy Bidelman: My earliest memories, as a toddler, were of always being in church. Every time those doors were open, we were there. We had such a very loving church family, and I have great memories of growing up. My parents were in their early thirties when I was a baby with two older brothers. We were very poor. My mom told me that when my brothers were little, they only had three shirts apiece. Whenever my dad was offered a raise, there was always a need somewhere in the church, so he would often decline the raise so that the church would have the money they needed. He would say, "God will provide for us." And he was right! It's amazing how something would always show up when we needed funds for a car repair or something like that. God always took care of our needs.

K. C. Armstrong: It sounds as though your faith was strong from the start.

Kathy Bidelman: That's how I was raised. I can remember as a four year old, my mother reading me a story about Jesus dying on the cross for our sins. She told me that if we accept Jesus into our hearts, we can go to Heaven someday. I asked her, "Is that where you're gonna be, Mom?" She prayed with me and I asked Jesus into my heart with the faith of a child. From that point on, no matter how much I messed up, I knew my eternity is set because my home is in Heaven. I did, however, go through the normal teenage years.

K. C. Armstrong: What about pressure? I mean, my father was a wrestling and football coach. I thought I had pressure! Did you feel that you had to be the perfect example of what your father was preaching?

Kathy Bidelman: Well, there was this thing that people would say: "Oh, the preachers' kids are the worst." So yeah, there was pressure to be a good example. Through my teen years I wasn't as close to the Lord as I should have been. There were times that I just went through the motions and periods of time when I strayed off course. But I've always, always come back, and God has always forgiven.

I was pretty sheltered because I did go to a Christian school. As I was growing up, I wasn't allowed to go to the movies or to dances. There wasn't much I was allowed to do. I tried a cigarette one time, but that was enough for me. Never did I try any drugs. I do remember being with friends and having a drink a few times, and I knew it wasn't right, that I shouldn't be doing that. So yes, I did stray a bit when others were testing the rules. There weren't any dances at the Christian school I went to, but I do have to admit I snuck out a few times to an under twenty-one dance when I was supposed to be "with a friend."

K. C. Armstrong: Right! I know how that works! You said you were going to sleep over someone's house…

Kathy Bidelman: You got it! It was completely harmless. My friends were allowed to go but because I was a pastor's kid, my parents wouldn't let me.

K. C. Armstrong: I appreciate your honesty, Kathy. As I've told you, my father was a very strict coach. At some point I got really fed up with all the rules and wanted to do the things that all the other kids were doing. I think most kids go through that.

Kathy Bidelman: I did feel like I was missing out on some normal things that my friends were allowed to do. But God protected me from some pitfalls, probably because I wasn't allowed to do those things. I wasn't allowed to date until I turned sixteen, and of course the guy had to be approved by my mom and dad. Actually, my dating experience was very limited and I married the first guy I ever dated.

K. C. Armstrong: Can you remember the first time that he came to pick you up and your father met him?

Kathy Bidelman: Oh yes! he was very charming with my parents, so that definitely helped. I was worried about what my parents would think, but he passed their scrutiny with flying colors, so it was all good.

K. C. Armstrong: How long did you guys date? Did you fall in love?

Kathy Bidelman: Well, I was sixteen. I don't think you would call it love, more like infatuation. I knew him only seven months before we married. We were both kids, and I don't think we had the time or maturity to develop a real relationship. I had never dated before. I got pregnant at sixteen, married, and had two sons by the age of eighteen.

K. C. Armstrong: How did your parents react to all this? You were, after all, still in high school.

Kathy Bidelman: First of all, being a preacher's kid, getting pregnant was embarrassing. Parents then weren't as open with kids as today, so I was naive and I made a mistake. My parents didn't force us to get married, but they made us feel that it was the right thing to do. I told my mom when we were away on vacation and my dad was at a conference. She advised me not to tell him until we all got back home. But my parents are the most loving and forgiving people, and they realized that we wanted to get married and raise our child for the Lord. So we did; we got married in November, the month I turned seventeen. My husband was nineteen. Happily, the Christian community and my husband's family all got behind us.

K. C. Armstrong: That's reassuring because people can be so judgmental. But you two took responsibility and did the best you could. And—fast forward—that first baby was Shane, who just received his PhD from Purdue University in chemical engineering, right?

Kathy Bidelman: Smart child I had when I was seventeen!

K. C. Armstrong: Did you manage to stay in school after Shane's birth?

Kathy Bidelman: No, I quit and then, as soon as my class graduated, I got my G.E.D immediately. I was slated to be Valedictorian of my class too, only a class of eighteen, but still I had the highest grades. I just felt that I needed to remove myself and make it less awkward for the Christian school as well as myself and my family.

K. C. Armstrong: You had to "remove" yourself? How did you feel about that?

Kathy Bidelman: Well, I felt I let my parents down. I really did. They were always loving and forgiving, but I did feel I let them down. I had goals too; I had wanted to go to school to be a teacher. I had even picked out a college, but the pregnancy changed everything. I would not trade my kids for the world, of course, but at the time I was disappointed in myself, that I made a mistake.

K. C. Armstrong: Well sure, at sixteen you still want to please your parents and your teachers, and at the same time you're developing dreams for your own future. I can just imagine, as a young, inexperienced girl, making one mistake that turns your entire life upside down, but in an amazing way. You talk openly about your personal struggles. Do you think God uses you to uplift other people with how you've been able to work through these challenges?

Kathy Bidelman: Yes, absolutely. I believe God uses the things that we go through in our life to help others in the future. As a result of what I've been through, I've been able to encourage and uplift others that are going through their own set of problems. I put a lot of inspirational posts on Facebook, and I share my devotionals and such. Many times what I post is like what I've gone through, what I've needed for myself that God gave to me. I just want to share what's helped me. I'm not trying to preach.

K. C. Armstrong: Once you got married and had this wonderful little Shane, what was your life like?

Kathy Bidelman: My husband was an x-ray technician and made only $8.00 an hour. We were poor and received food stamps, and that wasn't the only time in our lives we struggled financially.

However, we had a great support system. Both of our parents were very young still and helped us in every way they could. But we were also just kids ourselves. So it was like we were raised together. I feel like we never really had a normal relationship; we were almost like brother and sister, which is not the way to develop a strong marital relationship with each other.

But you know, K. C., I chose to love him. I chose to be committed to the church, my parents, and my whole family. They all made it easy to stay in that condition for so long. The infatuation did turn into a kind of love, but not typical spousal love. Even though we went through a divorce, we have three kids together and we are good friends to this day. We're supportive of each other and our kids.

K. C. Armstrong: It's great that you guys are friends. It obviously was a great thing for the kids. If I could brag to the audience here, Shane received his PhD from Purdue. Nathan was announced Valedictorian at his high school graduation and married the girl of his dreams, Amanda. Did your religious faith contribute to your becoming such a good parent that you could show your kids how to deal with challenges to become successful?

Kathy Bidelman: I believe so. When I was walking closer to the Lord, of course, everything was easier. When my boys were young, before my first daughter came along, things were just so much simpler. There were no cell phones or anything like that. It was all about family and doing things together, like family game nights. So I do feel that faith got us through those years. Definitely.

K. C. Armstrong: Kathy, I think we have a pretty clear view of your life growing up. You were raised in the church with loads of support from your family and church community. For the most part, you stayed true to the beliefs of your religion. You married and gave birth to your first child at the age of sixteen. We can understand that you are a loving, religious person who tries to do the right thing by God and others.

I know this is difficult for you, but I'm going to ask now about a life altering event. Can you tell us what happened to your family in 1984?

Kathy Bidelman: When I was fifteen years old, my ten year old brother and I attended a small Christian school and rode the

> *Looking up at the end of the service, I saw my dad hugging the man that killed my little brother, and they were both sobbing.*

same bus each day. Even though I got off the bus first, Stevie always liked to race me to the house. One particular day I was more dressed up than usual. My friend and I were wearing matching dresses to sing in front of the church group, and I was even wearing high heels.

As we climbed off the school bus, I was about to tell Stevie that I wasn't racing that day, but he darted around me and across the road. Someone in a pickup truck was in a hurry, did not stop behind the bus, attempted to pass, and hit my brother—only four feet in front of me. He went down in a pool of blood just steps away. Although most of that day is a blur, I remember screaming and dropping to the ground in shock. My mom came running out of the house after she heard me scream. I don't remember too much, but I was at my neighbors' house while my parents were at the hospital.

During the early days after the accident there was a little hope because Stevie would squeeze a hand very slightly. This gave us hope that he was hearing us and responding. It was so hard seeing my brother lying there in a coma. The swelling in his brain was critical, and he had to have surgeries to remove the pressure. His lungs were also heavily damaged, and he had several broken bones. My parents were at the hospital every day, but in ICU there were only certain times we could see him. Because there was a great risk of infection to him, my parents had to wear masks and sterile gowns to go into his room, and I was rarely allowed in to see him. The staff at the hospital and all the people at church were so supportive of us through all this.

My parents were and are loved by so many. But now, being a mom myself, I can't imagine how heartbreaking this was for them. I have four kids, and I don't know how they could get through pain like that. Now that I've experienced the love you have for your own child, I realize how it must have ripped their hearts out every day. I know their faith got them through, but my faith as a teen was not as strong. I didn't understand how God would let this happen. I was angry and bitter. After fifty-four days in a coma, Stevie died.

At Stevie's Memorial Service a few days later, the church was packed. So many people spoke, and I remember sitting up front with my family and crying while the congregation sang "Great is Thy Faithfulness." I felt numb inside.

K. C. Armstrong: I'm so sorry, Kathy. That must have been devastating for all of you.

Kathy Bidelman: Thank you, K. C. I just couldn't understand why God would allow my brother to die. Stevie had just told my dad a few months earlier that he wanted to be a pastor, just like him. I did question God. My parents knew that I internalized a lot of pain and carried it around with me for a long time before I could finally forgive.

K. C. Armstrong: And yet, Kathy, you witnessed such an incredible example of forgiveness at this time. Please tell us about the most remarkable thing you saw after your brother's service.

Kathy Bidelman: Looking up at the end of the service, I saw my dad hugging the man that killed my little brother, and they were both sobbing. I heard my father say that he and my mom had forgiven him, the man who took their son's life. At the time I couldn't understand it. I didn't feel it. My parents even decided not to press any additional charges or go after this man, who only got a thirty day license suspension and a $100 fine for what he did. But I realize now that forgiveness is a choice—a deliberate act of love, mercy and grace—a deliberate act not to hold something against another person no matter what they have done to you. This is the forgiveness my parents showed to the man who killed my little brother.

Even with such an example, it took me a really long time to forgive, and I carried that anger through my adult years until something really incredible happened. In the year 2008, I became postmaster in

12

a small town called Tire Hill, and three houses down from the Post Office lived the widow of the man who had killed my brother.

All these years later, God placed me in this little post office in a small town just a short walk from this woman, who by that time had lost her husband to cancer. The widow would come into the Post Office every day, and I got to know her. What an amazing person she is! She's eighty-seven now and has served in her church for years and years. She takes communion to shut-ins, served in hospice, and sang in her church choir. I often wonder what her life would be like if my parents had not forgiven her husband. Would she be serving in her church bringing relief to so many people, or would she have passed away an angry, bitter woman? You can't know, but I believe in a ripple effect. When we make the hard choice to forgive, we've taken the burden off ourselves and we help others. Think of the effect my parents' act of forgiveness made on so many lives!

This woman and I ended up being friends, hugging and crying together. My dad lives just up the road and he runs into her, as well. We may not know what the eternal consequences will be until we're in Heaven, but we all chose forgiveness. The Bible says in Romans 8:28, "God works for the good of those who love Him and who have been called according to His purpose."

That doesn't mean that everything is necessarily going to be great, but it means that everything that happens to us will end up producing goodness somehow. God is molding us and maybe preparing us to be able to comfort somebody else that is going through the same type of thing one day.

K. C. Armstrong: Kathy, how did your outlook on life evolve through this experience?

Kathy Bidelman: To be honest, it took a long while for me to work through all this and finally forgive that driver. Meeting his wife made a huge difference. Also, my dad preached a message once in a while on bitterness. He would say, "There is only one letter difference between BITTER and BETTER. If you choose to be BITTER, then the "I" is on the throne... but if you choose BETTER, the "E" for *Emmanuel* [the Messiah] is on the throne." My parents let this horrifying experience make them BETTER and not BITTER! Their attitude of acceptance has been the truest and best earthly example to me. God's forgiveness to us is the ultimate example.

Through my brother Stevie's death, I learned that we need to forgive. When we do, we take the burden off ourselves. My family knows that we're going to see Stevie again because when he was just four or five years old he asked Jesus into his heart, so he will be with Jesus for eternity.

I have since had more reason to dig deeply into the well of forgiveness. I think of the thief on the Cross on Mount Calvary, who found belief in Jesus just before he died. Jesus said, "Today you will be with me in Paradise." Ours is a God of second chances, wanting everyone to be saved, offering His forgiveness to all who put their faith and trust in Him.

K. C. Armstrong: Kathy, this has been such an overwhelming experience, beginning in tragedy but also leading to emotional and religious growth. What would you like others to take from your story?

Kathy Bidelman: Mostly that forgiveness is a gift that God extends to us, and when we forgive others, it is so freeing. The burden is lifted. Even if the person who hurt us never says they are sorry, we have made the choice to become *BETTER*, not *BITTER*.

The remarkable example of my parents has illustrated this theme. When we go through misfortune, God uses that experience to help us comfort or encourage others going through the loss of a child or family member or other devastation. I also want to mention something that came out of this, as well. As a result of Stevie's accident, stricter laws and penalties for passing a bus have been enacted. Stop signs and bars coming out from the buses have been added.

K. C. Armstrong: Thank you so much, Kathy, for spending this time with us and for your honesty. I know this can't be easy to discuss. I'm sure you've helped a lot of people today and provoked them to think about forgiveness as a *choice* that we all have. It's easy to hate or to hold a grudge. That doesn't make us feel better, but it makes us feel justified, I guess.

I am also absolutely amazed at your parents' ability to live their Christian values and show us all how beneficial love and compassion are for us and our families, and how that spirals off to others. You are simply an amazing woman, and I will try to think of one person in my life today that I can practice forgiveness on.

Kathy Bidelman: Great, K. C.! Remember, forgiveness is a choice! Your first concern should be to receive the freedom from who's hurt you or what has happened. Your feelings will follow in time, once you have made that decision.

K. C. Armstrong: Incredible advice, Kathy! It's interesting that we are here in a soundproof room, but there are fireworks going on outside—and for some reason I can hear them on my headphones! I'm not sure what is happening, but I feel like I am hearing applause for your amazing inspiration! I'm proud to call you my friend, and one of the *World's Most Amazing Women,* Kathy Bidelman.

More information about Kathy:

Facebook: https://www.facebook.com/kathy.bidelman.5

A WOMAN'S VOICE

an interview with Cicilia Seleyian

*Cicilia grew from a powerless Kenyan girl-child to an
international spokesperson for gender equality.*

INTRODUCTION:

I learned a long time ago that it is OK to ask questions, but it's wrong
and disrespectful to be close-minded. It's arrogant to listen to the
way someone else lives and to react in a way that passively insults and
dismisses their way of life.

I've met Cicilia Seleyian many times and seen for myself how kind,
bright and loyal she is. Cicilia travels to the U.S. and stays at my
Mom's house while she educates American school kids about distant
cultures. While in the schools and other speaking venues, she sells
jewelry handmade by the women of her village for the benefit of
women's issues, including school fees, food and clean water.

During this interview I wasn't comfortable with customs she described, which I judged to be demeaning to women. I was brought up to believe in equal abilities and opportunities between genders. The problem is, instead of just listening to Cicilia's traditions, I judged them by comparing them to my own.

I can see that we actually cause division when we believe that what we have been taught is the only way to do things. I admire Cicilia so much for working within the structure of her society to make positive changes in health, education and gender equality.

I know that Cicilia's traditions are strong. I know firsthand her dedication to her family and her community. The society that raised her instilled in her a character of honesty, respect and fairness. She is able to sort the valuable wisdom of an ancient tribe that has prospered throughout history from the traditions that are outdated. She is a true hero in my opinion.

INTERVIEW:

K. C. Armstrong: Though it is midnight here in New York, I am speaking to a beautiful Maasai woman who is having breakfast with her family over 7,000 miles away. Cicilia Seleyian and her husband, Chief Joseph ole Tipanko, are members of the East African Maasai tribes, which are located in Kenya and Tanzania, East Africa. Cicilia and the Chief have visited our WMAP station in New York several times during their visits to the U.S., but today I am speaking to Cicilia at her home in the Ngong Valley where she is sitting with her four month old son on her lap. It is in this home that her work for the global empowerment of women originated and evolved. It's my pleasure and my great honor to introduce Cicilia Seleyian. Miss Cecilia, so good to speak with you today.

Cicilia Seleyian: Thank you so much, K. C. I'm very happy to be talking to you and to be sharing with you about my career and about the Maasai women.

K. C. Armstrong: I'm glad we're finally able to make a connection. A book about amazing women would not be complete without you, Cicilia. I know you are a member of the oldest indigenous culture in Africa and that your traditions and culture date back to ancient times. Since you have traveled here many times, you know that we in the US live a very different life from you. With your husband and other cultural ambassadors, you have literally seen both sides of the world and cultures that could hardly be more different. And yet in some ways we all really seek the same things in life. If you would, please tell our readers a little about your life as a young Maasai girl.

Cicilia Seleyian: Sure. I was born in 1976 at Oloitokitok village on the footsteps of Mt. Kilimanjaro, which borders Kenya and Tanzania. As a young girl I was raised in the Maasai cultural lifestyle and made to observe the ancient Maasai traditions. For a woman that means collecting firewood, fetching water, cooking, beading, child raising, and initiation in preparation for motherhood. I was lucky to get a basic elementary education at Inkisanchani primary school. I wasn't able to proceed to high school however, due to lack of school tuition fees and the Maasai way of life that devalues the girl child in the society compared to the boy child.

Even today, the girl is treated simply as an asset to earn the family wealth in the form of dowry: cows, blankets, and local brew for the elders. It is not thought important for the girl to get a school education. My father married four wives, and I am the second child of the eldest wife. Being raised in a polygamous family was not easy due to competition of the scarce family resources for a better life. Supporting four wives is a sign of power and wealth, but educating seventeen children was not easy for my dad. The boy child is always favored in terms of education while the girl is married off in her teenage years, even to an older man. The man could be age about forty years, but she does not have a choice of whom she will marry. My dad was treated as a brave man in his youth, having killed a lion and being from the Irmolelian clan. He was treated as a strong man because raising and feeding a large family defines the man's social status.

K. C. Armstrong: You said girls were married in their teens, but they may marry a man as old as forty. I suppose these are arranged marriages?

Cicilia Seleyian: That is true. In my culture, girls do not have a choice of the man they will marry. Our parents say, "This is the man I want you to marry," and we respect our parents' wisdom. First, the man approaches the girl's parents who can say yes or no to a proposed marriage. They look at the man's character and whether he has wealth in the form of cows and blankets. Maasai girls are only important because of the dowry they will be able to bring to the family when they marry.

K. C. Armstrong: What happens if a girl favors a man she sees in her village? Can she date him?

Cicilia Seleyian: Since our parents choose our husbands, no, we do not have a right to date. A girl could go to her mother and say, "Madam, I like this man. Is this OK for me to marry?" The mother has the right to say yes or no. She would look at the man's character and she can say, "For me, I don't like this and this and this…" or "you love him—but for me, I don't like." We respect our elders and our traditions, so we listen to what our mothers tell us.

K. C. Armstrong: How do these arranged marriages work out? What do you do if you don't get along?

Cicilia Seleyian: Before I got married, my mother told me, "When you disagree with your husband, don't come to me. Go to your mother-in-law; don't come to my home." So if there are problems, a wife should go to her mother-in-law, and the husband can go to the elders for advice. We do not have divorce.

K. C. Armstrong: Tell us more about growing up in Oloitokitok Village.

Cicilia Seleyian: As a Maasai girl, female genital mutilation was inevitable during my early years. Though it is painful and even dangerous, I had no choice. The older women called me early one morning and said it was time that I have to be a woman and not a girl any more. Together they pinned me on the ground, and a crude knife and razor blade befell my body. I was helpless as I screamed at the top of my voice with no help. Something so painful I will never forget.

K. C. Armstrong: This is the rite of becoming a woman which is referred to as "FGM." Is this still practiced in the Maasai community today?

Cicilia Seleyian: Yes, typically at around nine years old. It is one of the important things I am trying to educate my people about. Girls have so much pain and bleeding, sometimes for days. This is not necessary anymore, and we are trying to make changes. But it is hard for old people to understand why we are stopping the old practices.

K. C. Armstrong: Your husband is a Maasai chief. Can't he forbid the practice?

Cicilia Seleyian: No. He is not the chief of government but Chief of tradition. He must work through the elders to change old traditions, and that takes much time and effort. The older tribal members do not want to change the ways they have followed for so many ages. A lot of what my husband teaches is through example. I am his only wife, for instance.

K. C. Armstrong: Cicilia, we talked about marriage in general, but tell us how your marriage to Chief Joseph came about.

Cicilia Seleyian: A young skinny warrior came to my village from 300 kilometers away [about 186 miles]. He tells me he saw a beautiful girl in the village, and so he went to my parents and proposed marriage. My parents agreed and they said, "This is your husband," without asking me because it is the rule for them to decide. My parents knew he was the Chief of his age group and could support me. Later, his parents visited my home and a marriage negotiation was discussed and arranged. We are now happily married with five children. I am lucky because he is a good man and we work well together.

K. C. Armstrong: Nice! I've seen you two together, and I can tell Chief Joseph has great respect for you and your opinions.

Cicilia Seleyian: He is very helpful and involved in my work of bringing a voice to the women of our community. Most women here do not have a say about anything at all. I am a mother and housewife but I am also the chairperson of a women's group advocating for women empowerment and rights for women and girls. Our goals are to have good health, education and participation in community development issues.

As a Maasai lady who has grown in harsh and cruel environments that overlook the rights of women and girls, my prayer is to speak and advocate for issues that affect women. To speak for women's rights for a better future: better education, good health, equality and economic and social empowerment. I would love to see women being respected, honored and valued in all aspects of life as able and equal achievers. And I would love to see their efforts appreciated as contributors in nation building. In my community, Joseph can suggest to the Elders to give the women power through education and bead work and school for the girls. I believe that when we educate our girls we educate the whole world. However, the traditional Maasai, especially the men, do not see the need for change.

We tell our parents that education makes the girl like the boy. A woman's small business in the community can help the man by paying school fees, buying books, and even buying clothes and food to help the man support his family.

K. C. Armstrong: What are the traditional roles in the Maasai family?

Cicilia Seleyian: First of all, milk and meat are our traditional food. A Maasai without cows is looked at as useless. If you do not drink blood or milk, you are not a Maasai. Part of our traditional work is for the women to build the houses, not the men. We collect mud, sticks and cow dung and mix them together for the boma [hut]. When it is raining and the house is leaking, even in the middle of the night, the woman must wake up and get the cow dung and plaster the leaking areas. At that time the man is still sleeping. The man is the security of the village and the house and the breadwinner.

We do not have running water for washing and drinking, and the woman must seek water. We walk seven km [about 4.5 miles] each way and carry twenty gallons on our backs to bring home. We do not have machines anywhere so all the work is done with our hands. We also don't have electricity and use firewood instead. Even our kids use firewood for doing studying or homework.

We women don't allow our men to go to the kitchen. They would not know what to do! Even when a woman is sick, the man goes to another home to call a woman to come and help him and cook for him. So that is the work the women do in the village.

Also, in our culture when women bring the food to the men, they go out because they should not see a man when he eats. When I bring the meal to my husband, I leave and when he ceases eating I return. Even now, the old men can not sit together with the children. When old men come to the house to visit, the children cannot stay. They must leave.

The order of importance in Maasailand is first, the cow. Second, the man. Third, the boy. And last, the girls and women.

K. C. Armstrong: Is it true that the men must kill a lion as a rite of passage?

Cicilia Seleyian: Traditionally, yes. Boys must become men through circumcision to become warriors. From individual kills, the boys would now go instead in age groups to kill lions, never a female. But now in many cases this is banned by the government.

K. C. Armstrong: With all the work that you do and all the restrictions put upon you by your society, you have still become an activist for women's rights in Maasailand. How do you go about empowering women?

Cicilia Seleyian: When I travel I see different cultures with a lot of things: running water, electricity, food and big houses. When you come to Maasailand, things are totally different. Because of our history and traditions, women and girls have no worth. The order of importance in Maasailand is first, the cow. Second, the man. Third, the boy. And last, the girls and women. We have no voice or opinion. I am told that because I am a lady I am a useless person with no worth, and I cannot be anything in the community. This is what I want to change. We all are capable of work and have value. Many of our women bead jewelry and clothing to sell to help their families afford the necessities of life.

K. C. Armstrong: What are you doing to improve life for the women in your Maasai community?

Cicilia Seleyian: I am now protecting thirty girls who have run to me because they do not want to be cut. I have gone to their parents and told them the problems with FGM. I take these girls to school so we educate them, including the value of avoiding FGM. We teach the young ladies to understand the need for this change for the sake of their own health and their children. That is our work now. Some elders even give workshops to teach about FGM.

My work is also to provide education for the girls and good clean water for the community. We have a lot of problems with animals while our girls go to fetch water in terms of safety and also pollution of the water.

When I first traveled to the U.S. I spoke at a United Nations conference on women's rights and issues that affect women and how to address them. Many people in my community could not believe I could do that, especially the men. But together they were amazed when I traveled and I was able to bring home more scholarship support for our young Maasai girls—laptops for the schools, and funds to dig a water well and to build a safe house dormitory. The walls to the dormitory are up, and we just need the roof, bedding and other supplies for our rescued teenage school girls. The dorm, when completed, will be able to house up to sixty girls from child trafficking and bad Maasai traditions like female genital cutting, early girl child marriage, and the fangs of poverty that exploit children, especially the girls. Instead, the girls will be unharmed, have supervision in a safe house, and go to school.

K. C. Armstrong: Cecilia, this work that you are doing is so important for the entire community, but it threatens the older people who do not want to see the culture change. Do you ever feel threatened?

Cicilia Seleyian: Sure. A lot of men tell me that a woman does not have the right to speak and be heard in our community. Other men have come to my husband and told him to get another lady. But my husband understands me because he is educated, so we sit down and do work together. The elders say, "You want to be like a man, but you are not. You are still a woman."

Even though there is resistance within, a lot of people outside the country understand and listen to what I am doing to see that our girls and women have rights. We now have seven schools, and more Maasai people are giving their girls permission to go to school. People are starting to understand that education is important for both girls and boys. Change comes slowly, but the community is seeing progress.

K. C. Armstrong: How are you able to fund your schools and women's programs?

Cicilia Seleyian: People outside our country have been generous in helping us develop our programs. The Chief, myself, and two other Cultural Ambassadors make trips to other countries where we present programs to share our ancient culture while fundraising for schools and scholarships. We are able to help many of our children attend school regularly. And we provide as many scholarships as possible for poor girls and those who escape FGM by coming to myself and the Chief. We put these girls, many of whom are disowned by their families, in boarding schools. Now that we are building a dormitory for them to stay, they will be in our local school where we can watch over them. The result is that they can get jobs when they graduate and help their families financially. The families of disowned girls often take the girls back when they see that an educated girl can contribute to their families in ways other than just providing dowries.

Our women provide beaded clothing and jewelry for our trips to the U.S. We sell the items and return all the proceeds to the women to use for their families. This is kept separate from the money we earn for education and community building. More and more people are seeing what we have been able to do through education and also through our fundraising. We have finished our well and are just waiting for enough new funding to provide a solar-powered generator. We have sponsors for our thirty girls but have to continually fund raise while in the States to maintain the help for these girls until they graduate. We help as many girls as we can, within our budget.

My wish is to see our programs expand to a point where we will be able to sustain ourselves instead of relying on the generosity of our friends around the world. Our educated women will create small businesses which can then help their families. The Maasai traditional way of life is changing, and we can not rely only on our herds of cattle, goats and sheep to support our tribes. With climate change and the need for our children to attend school, as well as shrinking Maasai territory, we must make some adaptations to the present day.

K. C. Armstrong: Cicilia, you were born into a Maasai family of one man, four wives, and seventeen children. You have experienced the beauty and the scars of Maasai culture. We haven't even discussed the strength of Maasai values which are so beautiful—reverence for the elders, the bonds of the family, the importance of peace, honesty and integrity. I certainly hope those values are never lost and that we can discuss those valuable pieces of the Maasai culture in another book. But for now, we celebrate you for the amazing advocacy of women all around the world—someone who is making a real difference for her community. What thoughts would you like to leave with our readers?

Cicilia Seleyian: I would like to invite people to join me in empowering the women in their own communities. Every woman in the whole world should have a voice that is heard. Women and men are equally capable of good work, and both should be valued and recognized for their worth.

K. C. Armstrong: Cicilia, you are a courageous warrior yourself, fighting for the rights of women everywhere. We are so grateful for your work and your time in sharing what you are doing in Maasailand and around the world. We at WMAP value you, we hear your voice, and we honor you as one of the *World's Most Amazing Women.*

More information about Cicilia:

Website: https://magsaoutreach.org/
Note: For information on Maasai U.S. presentations, visit www.leavingfootprints.org.

RECOVERY

an interview with Debra Morgan

Debra Morgan had the courage to recover from a troubled childhood and chemical addiction to help others find their own inner strength

INTRODUCTION:

I spent a lot of time with Debra Morgan and was moved by her courage in the face of emotional abuse. Hers is a story that any of you who struggle with addiction, or love someone who does, can applaud and cheer because—in this case—we got a win. Debra is so impressive because she did what most addicts don't do until it's too late. She had the guts to peel back the layers of emotional abuse and a lifetime of being deceived. Even after developing fibromyalgia, Debra held strong against returning to the self-destructive potential of prescription medications. This is a deep and growing social problem that touches us all. Debra's example shows us that we can keep digging within ourselves to find a way to escape our torments and addictions. This is a chapter you may want to share with someone you know who needs some hope and guidance.

INTERVIEW:

K. C. Armstrong: Guys, I want to tell you right now, I have an amazing guest! Debra Morgan is an author, blogger, and also a recovering addict. Debra has an amazing story which can help us understand people in our own lives who have suffered this particular agony. Unfortunately, addiction is a problem that isn't going away, and Debra has publicized her success story to help other people create and maintain their own recovery. So guys, with no further ado, it is my honor and pleasure to introduce Debra Morgan. Welcome, Debra, and thank you for your courage and honesty in discussing this sensitive topic with us today.

Debra Morgan: Thank you, K. C. Actually, *honesty* is something that took me a long time to learn. We were never honest in our family; growing up was one big lie after another. Seeking the truth was a huge issue in my childhood, in my growth, and in my need to feel "normal."

K. C. Armstrong: Debra, part of the dishonesty you mention is being raised by your grandmother and having to tell everybody that your mother was your sister. What on earth was that about?

Debra Morgan: Well, it's funny. I still have the first picture I ever saw of myself. On one side of the photo is my grandma holding me, and on the other side is my mom. That's the way I can best describe my life. Both of them were always present, but their roles were reversed. Either my mom gave me away to my grandma, or there was a theft by my grandma from my mom. I never knew what really happened back then; I was an infant. But the result was that I was raised to believe I was the daughter of my grandmother, making me my actual mother's "sister."

To complicate matters even further, when my mom continued to have kids, they became my "nieces" instead of my sisters. I know, it's confusing; you have to think about that a bit. This habitual pattern of deception was the foundation of my life from the very beginning.

K. C. Armstrong: So you were conditioned to lie because the truth would get you into trouble with your family. I guess there had to be confusion and anger in having to live a lie of that magnitude. You told us that you started drinking very early and later got into drugs, beginning with marijuana. Is there a relationship between that and the unusual demands at home?

Debra Morgan: Oh yeah. I began drinking at twelve, out of rebellion. When I was young, I was sick constantly and out of school all the time. Who knows whether I was really sick or just miserable from nerves or anxiety? Every house has its problems and secrets, but not like somebody impersonating one of your parents every day. My great grandma lived with us as well, and she was the one that actually kept me going.

K. C. Armstrong: Where was your father when all this was going on?

Debra Morgan: I didn't meet my father until I was twenty-four. My grandma had always kept him completely away from me and would not even accept child support payments, so he would have no contact. When I was six years old, they told me he was in town and would probably try to kidnap me. I couldn't play in the front yard for two months. I'd be taken to school and brought right home afterwards, and I was in lock down while in school. Nobody else could pick me up, and I felt like a prisoner.

As a kid I was very lonely. You get to the point where your friends on the street become your family. As you get older, you want to be out of the house whenever you can. Everything I started doing from when I was twelve years old was meant as payback to my grandmother and my mom. Anything I could do to make them mad or frustrated—that's what I did. I was a devil and just wanted to get even for all the frustration and pain they caused me.

Sometimes my grandma would try to ground me, but the worst punishment she gave me affected me very deeply. I was a track runner and I was going to the state meet that year, which really meant a lot to me. But after I was involved in a drinking episode in front of the school, my grandma told me that I couldn't go back to track. Everybody, including my coach, tried to talk her into relenting, but she wouldn't do it. From that point on, there was no turning back for me. I decided that if she wasn't going to let me participate in the only thing that I felt good about, then she would get what she deserved. So at that point things changed, and I let my hostility show openly.

K. C. Armstrong: What a terrible mistake on her part! There was one thing that gave you some identity and self-confidence, and she took it away.

Debra Morgan: Right. There was nothing left to take any pride in. Nothing. My team didn't understand what was going on. How could they? It made no sense. They knew I lived with my grandma, but they knew I had a mom, too. Nobody got it.

K. C. Armstrong: Incredible, Deb. So I can see how this resulted in your moving out as soon as you were able.

Debra Morgan: Right. I started dating a guy from school who had always wanted to date me. At the time, he felt like somebody who cared about me and who I could rely on. I ended up pregnant, still only seventeen years old. I wanted to keep the baby, but my grandmother absolutely forbade it. She was strongly against abortion, but she was more afraid of a blight on her reputation.

Again, it was all about her. She said, "You're too young. We're going to set up an appointment," and she did. As before, I had no input into what was happening in my life. Guess what I got in return for having an abortion? A dog. I'm not joking. I ended up with a puppy. That was supposed to replace what I had just gone through emotionally and physically. One of the most important decisions of my life, and it was taken out of my hands.

K. C. Armstrong: What does something like that do to a woman?

Debra Morgan: There's a deep emptiness. I don't know if it ever goes away. By the time I was twenty-one I had met and married someone after a short engagement. When our daughter was born, I finally had somebody to love and take care of, someone who was going to need me, and that was a big deal. I always wanted to be a parent, and I was thrilled. Before long though, my marriage was faltering and I was having emotional issues. But I was being the best parent I could be, and my main goal was to keep my daughter safe and happy.

As my marriage fell apart, I moved in with the guy I had dated in high school who had gotten me pregnant. He had always shown concern for me, and it seemed like we had known each other forever. I married him, but I didn't realize until too late that living with him was not the same as dating him in school. The relationship was okay in the beginning; I got pregnant with my second child, a son, and I was attending college. I wanted to be a nurse and was accepted into the local nursing program. Unexpectedly, my husband revealed that he would not watch the kids at night if I were to get my nursing credentials, so there was no point in continuing with classes. Here I was again with someone controlling me and taking away my choice, my self-determination.

I found out that everything we had was in his name, not in ours. The bank account, the apartment, my car—all registered solely in his name. I was trapped with no way to get any funds. Another low point, and I turned to drinking.

One night I watched the *Patty Duke Story* on TV about her bipolar disorder. I thought, "That's me" and realized I needed to get checked out. I saw a doctor, who confirmed the diagnosis, and at the end of the visit he put me on Prozac for bi-polar disorder.

K. C. Armstrong: Did this help, Debra?

Debra Morgan: All the Prozac did was mask some of the symptoms that I was having. I would cycle between mania and depression continuously throughout the day, never feeling like I was "normal." I had previously been put on pain pills (Percocet) after a surgery, and it got to a point where I began to feel normal, or so I thought. That's when the addict's behavior kicked in. It's almost like somebody pushes a button. You don't just take a pill and turn into an addict; that is not how it works. Many people can be on drugs for years without becoming addicted, but I wasn't one of those people. At that point I was somehow broken inside.

So I began stealing prescription pads from doctors' offices. They weren't hard to get; doctors would leave them in the room during checkups when they went out to order tests or check on other things. At that time there were no watermarks or fax machines for security. I would write prescriptions under tons of different names. You see, it's not just the drugs that make someone an addict. It's as much about the behavior that develops. It's like you flip the switch and immediately you start to become somebody different. You get the guts to try something once, and if you don't get caught, you do it again. To get money for pills, I would take something off a store shelf and return it for cash. Addicts are the fastest liars in the world; they lie so quickly that people immediately believe what they say because it comes right out of their mouths seemingly without a second thought.

K. C. Armstrong: And when you're raised by a family that has taught you to lie your whole life, I'm sure you had a head start.

Debra Morgan: Right. The days were a constant battle to get enough pills. You wake up in the morning and go to the first stash of pills in a drawer. Five bottles. You might have them hidden everywhere like an alcoholic does with a bottle of alcohol. A lot of times they'd be hidden in the garage. It's a full-time job to make sure that you have enough pills to get you through the week. And then you're going to need enough to get you through the next week. I was taking 100 a week, and it was exhausting.

When you're writing prescriptions, you have to know exactly what you're doing. I could write in six different hand writings, changing from one doctor to another. People who have bi-polar disorder or people who are addicts are not stupid. It's almost like learning a trade: you learn how to write scripts. You learn how to pass them. I was not afraid.

K. C. Armstrong: I imagine at some point you were discovered.

Debra Morgan: Of course I got caught, and I was sent to rehab. After being weighed in, giving a urine sample and having my picture taken, I felt like I was going into prison. In a way I was. I was already living in a prison cell; I just didn't realize it. The first few days I looked around the room during group meetings and tried to figure people out. I was trying to get an idea of what I had to accomplish before I could be free.

Counselors started asking questions, and of course they expect you to be honest. When you first walk in there, all you have left is what I call a "cash register honesty," a phrase I've heard a million times through AA and other places. Basically, that means you're only honest to a point. You're not being deep down honest; you're only honest on the surface.

They showed me to my room which held two beds. I was the only one there when I checked in, but by the next day I had a roommate. The schedule was set up to let you know that you couldn't procrastinate; you had ten minutes to unpack your bags, ten minutes to get ready for a meeting. You got up in the morning at 6:00 am, which was a shock to me. You went right to breakfast where no caffeine was served. You came back and immediately went to a meeting.

My first meeting was relatively easy, and I thought, "Well, everybody else is talking, and it's not going to be that hard." But still, you have "the stinking thinking," meaning you haven't yet been on the hot seat to answer questions directed specifically to you. So you're sitting there thinking everything is going to be a cakewalk. They fed me this morning… I can get through this…

But then the counselor began to go around the room, asking every person what was going on with them. When he got to me, my arms were folded and I was scrunched up in the chair. He looked me in the eyes and said sternly, "You need to put your feet on the floor and unfold your arms."

K. C. Armstrong: What was the reason for that?

Debra Morgan: I believe he was making the point that for the time you were going to be there you would have to listen to these people and do whatever they told you. He said my body language suggested I would be holding things in. To allow myself to be truly open, I would have to have my arms completely unfolded with hands on my lap and feet flat on the floor! Without hesitation I said, "I can't." Those were the first words out of my mouth. "I can't."

He asked, "Why not?"

And I said, "Because my guts will fall out." I realized that's how I actually felt.

They went around the room and asked what our drug of choice was and what got us where we were. Of course two or three people were alcoholics, but when they got to the two anesthesiologists, I was shocked. Both of them were about to lose their licenses because of misuse of fentanyl, which is killing so many people today. Fentanyl is routinely given to patients after surgery to hold down the pain. It's administered as you're coming out of the anesthesia, and those doctors would siphon some off into needles, which they would take home and shoot into their own veins. Certain stories you don't forget, although you forget the names.

K. C. Armstrong: What were the days at your rehab like?

Debra Morgan: I had classes and classes and classes—all day long. I was allowed to go outside and even have smoke breaks. I'd have to ask when I wanted something to drink, and there were only two choices, orange juice and Hawaiian Punch. They had some recreational activities like ping pong, but there was no TV watching. It was pretty strict. By the time 8:30 at night came, I was tired.

When I had been there four or five days, they took us into a huge gym with a rock wall, the first I'd ever seen. I was strapped in and had to climb clear up to the top. Way up there was a thing that looked like a diving board, and I had to walk down to the far edge, turn around, and drop off the board backwards, trusting the people below to catch me! The activities that had anything to do with trust were the hardest for me but probably taught me the most. The staff continued to tear me down each day in preparation for helping me rebuild myself. Once I started to talk openly, I couldn't stop. The feelings seemed to spew out uncontrollably.

K. C. Armstrong: You had been protecting your secrets and emotions for a really long time.

Debra Morgan: Yes. I was amazed that when I told my story, people weren't shocked! Their stories were as bad as mine. You almost feel like you're home, in a way, but the goal of rehab was to hold a mirror in front of me. The only way I can explain it to people is that they break you into a million pieces, and then it's your responsibility to pick up the right pieces to put yourself back together again. When you leave there you won't be the same person who walked in, but you'll have all the best parts of you intact. The rest are left on the cutting room floor.

Some don't make it. We had one guy who just left. There was no fence. So he went out to the patio for a cigarette, and he just walked away. I was afraid because the rehab facility was the only place that I felt safe. You couldn't see your family except once a week during the evening, and there was only an hour for visitation. On Sundays they would invite the immediate family to come in although my grandmother (who raised me) would never come.

There came a day when I had the opportunity to go off campus for an hour during the day. I called my grandmother, who didn't live very far, so she brought me to her house. I was there for a half hour, and she barely spoke to me at all. Never asked me one question about rehab or anything. She felt that the whole "rehab thing" was me talking about her.

After the first half hour was up, I said, "I want you to take me back. I don't want to be here an hour. Just get me back." The rehab was now my safety zone, and I thought, "God, I hope the rest of my life is busy like this." By that time, I wanted to do what they were telling me. I was taken to AA meetings. I had no idea what an AA meeting was or what it would be like, but from my first night I felt welcome.

K. C. Armstrong: How had you left things with your husband when you went into rehab?

Debra Morgan: From the time the cops came to our door and confronted me about writing the prescriptions, our relationship wasn't good. Once I got home, I think our marriage lasted between three and five months.

Of course the kids were glad to see me, and fortunately our AA meetings offered a child-care program. My children could play with other kids whose parents were members and so became part of my recovery. I was so happy with that because I didn't want to ever lie to my kids about where I was and what I was doing. They could be involved and see for themselves what was going on.

I got a job that was going to have to feed and support myself and my two kids until I could get temporary custody and child support. I will never forget the magistrate at the custody hearing. He looked straight at me and said, "I'm going to have your husband pay support, but I do not believe that you are going to be able to make it."

When I heard that, whatever anger was left rose up and consumed me. I told my attorney that I needed to address the Court. I stood in front of the magistrate and I said, "Sir, I will take you up on that challenge. You won't see me here ever again because I *will* make it." And from that point forward I fought with everything I had, not just for my sobriety but for my kids, for my sanity, and to prove that magistrate wrong. I directed every bit of energy and strength I had to my sobriety so that I could prove I could support and raise my kids properly.

Ten years into recovery, I started including a better diet and lots of exercise into my routine. I worked with a trainer and felt really good. But later, all of a sudden, I realized I wasn't able to lift as much weight as I had been. After many tests, I was diagnosed with fibromyalgia. Nobody knows if it runs in the family, and there is only treatment, not a cure. I was suffering; even the shower water would hurt my body. The doctor said the only way to treat this was with pain medication and a muscle relaxant.

K. C. Armstrong: I can see the problem here. You worked so hard to overcome your addictions, and now the doctor was offering you more prescription drugs.

> *I absolutely believe that most people have more strength than they know they do.*

Debra Morgan: Exactly! What choice do you make? Do I live with that kind of pain, or do I risk another addiction? I didn't have that "cash register honesty" anymore because I'd learned that obviously wasn't the way to live. I truthfully explained to the doctor the full extent of my problems with Percocet and told him I would need to be closely monitored.

They put me on Vicodin, and I was able to handle it without asking for more or a stronger dose. I believe to this day that addiction is the breaking down of your soul; you just want to get away from your reality, feel better, and not think at all. I was shocked to see that I was able to handle the medication without relapsing, which was so totally off the mark from where I was thirteen years earlier. But I was a happier person than I had ever been before.

Eight years later, I had basically become disabled as a result of fibromyalgia. I found an acupuncturist to help me stay away from all the meds while also helping with the pain. I was determined to never go back to where I was, and I've kept that promise to myself to this day. Everything that happened at that point could have led me right back to where I started, but it didn't, and it won't.

K. C. Armstrong: So you kept the pain, but in return you got rid of the medication that they had prescribed for you?

Debra Morgan: That's right.

K. C. Armstrong: Addiction and fibromyalgia were both devastating to your body and your mind. For you to come off the medications because you know they are a danger to you, even though you still struggle with fibromyalgia pain, is really amazing.

Debra Morgan: Well, thank you. I'm so much happier today, and all I take now is tramadol. That's it. I think back and wonder, how did I have the strength to get through it all? I don't know. But I absolutely believe that most people have more strength than they know they do.

K. C. Armstrong: That's wonderful, Deb. We are so happy for you! Your life must have opened up tremendously. What kind of advice can you give someone going through something similar?

Debra Morgan: Looking back, every experience I went through taught me something, even when I wasn't paying attention. It was painful, but slowly I progressed to the wonderful life I'm living today. To someone going through the same sort of horrible journey, I think the first thing I'd say is to accept the fact that you have problems and that you need to talk about them. Find someone to listen to you, maybe a good therapist. Just keep in mind that unless you really want to get over drugs or alcohol, it's not going to happen. I know people say this all the time, but there's a world of difference between wanting to get clean and *really* wanting to get clean; it's the cash register honesty again. There's no way anybody can do the hard work, and it *is* hard, for you.

I hope people who know they have an addiction will face it head-on and start the process of finding help earlier than I did. There are people out there that will listen and guide you.

K. C. Armstrong: Can you describe, Deb, how sobriety has changed your life?

Debra Morgan: Confronting my battles has changed everything about my life, beginning with my outlook. I have been clean now for twenty-five years, even with the strong temptations to medicate my fibromyalgia. That could have reopened the whole nightmare of addiction, but I will fight against this disease while remaining clean. I have so much to be proud of. I moved to the top of my career until I had to stop for health reasons. I raised two great children and am a loving grandmother! I have no hate for those who hurt me and won't carry anger, which would only empower them. I have a wonderful marriage with blended families. My life has been changed, and I am so grateful.

Looking back, the only person who ever treated me with unconditional love was my great-grandmother. I know now that she saved me. She was the one person who made me feel somewhat safe, and I would like to be that one person for someone else.

K. C. Armstrong: And to do so, you are a regular blogger, author, and radio guest sharing your advocacy for mental health and recovery.

Debra Morgan: That's right. I can imagine the pain in others' lives knowing what I have been through. I would love to ease the way for others, to speed them on their journey of forgiveness and putting the fragments of their broken spirits together.

K. C. Armstrong: Debra, you're definitely an incredible, generous woman! There are so many people that fall into addictions and don't talk about them. Hearing your story and perhaps consulting your blogs or listening to you on the radio, could be helpful for someone who is trying to hide a secret and either beat their addiction alone or just give in to it. Thank you for talking candidly about your struggles and sharing your victory. It is this victory and your dedication to support and inform so many other people that we celebrate you as one of the *World's Most Amazing Women.*

More information about Deb:

Website: *Deb-spot.com*
Facebook Fan page: *Deb Spot*
Autobiography: *Trapped* (to be released 2020)

SURVIVAL

an interview with R. Jade McAuliffe

*Jade lived a nightmare and now helps other suicide loss
survivors to trust themselves and the world again.*

INTRODUCTION:

Jade dedicates her life to hope, healing and empowerment after suicide loss. This created an instant bond when I first met her. There is
an organization called "Out of the Darkness" which organizes thousands of people affected by suicide to walk from dusk til dawn in a
different city each year. The course is usually 17 miles, and the event
brings awareness to the tragedy of suicide, the second leading cause
of death in the world for ages 15-24 and the 10th leading cause of
death in the U.S. for all ages. Every day 123 Americans take their
own lives, which calculates to one death every 12 minutes or about
45,00 Americans every year. Jade knows this horror and works to
relieve the pain of those who are affected.

Jade joined her local suicide prevention as a co-chair of the 2017 Out of the Darkness Event, which I missed due to a hospitalization. I often joke to Jade about the time my old ass was doing the walk in San Francisco for Christina Rossi, when I had to take a couple hours break because I got lost (I was in the back) and couldn't find my group. If you have a chance to go to the yearly walk, I encourage you to do so to see for yourself the heartache left behind after suicide. It is so inspirational to witness how people lean on each other and support one another to make sense of something most won't ever understand.

Revealing Jade's story makes me so grateful for the opportunity to interview courageous individuals with stories that people otherwise would never hear—or believe. Her example gives hope and inspiration to us all.

INTERVIEW:

K. C. Armstrong: Our next guest is R. Jade McAuliffe, an author, life coach, poet, and the founder of *No Parameters*, an organization that supports women after trauma and loss. How are you today, Jade?

Jade McAuliffe: Fine! Thanks for having me on the show.

K. C. Armstrong: Our listeners are intrigued by your story. They want to know more, especially how you came out of your tragic background to become the successful person you are today. For those who haven't heard your story so far, could you give us a quick summary of your personal history?

Jade McAuliffe: OK, sure. I grew up in Southeast Wisconsin in an upper middle-class family with two older sisters and an older brother. My mother stayed at home to take care of the four of us while my father worked as a physician. Unfortunately, he was also physically, sexually, and psychologically abusive to us throughout our childhoods. We ended up being subjected to sadistic cult abuse, based on rituals meant to completely control us. Even though he was a respected and well-known doctor in our community, no one outside our house knew about the living nightmare he created for us. He basically used fear and mind-control to make us "behave."

K. C. Armstrong: That's terrible. If you can, tell us a little more so we can better understand who you are and how far you've come today.

Jade McAuliffe: Our father was not well, but nobody on the outside knew it. He was relatively affluent and admired in the community. Honestly, I couldn't have told you details of that tangled-up, confusing, hellish nightmare until I was in my twenties with kids of my own. I was forty before I figured out that we were abused in a group setting.

K. C. Armstrong: Do you mean you couldn't remember what happened to you and your siblings until you became a young adult?

Jade McAuliffe: That's right, and it took decades of therapy to make sense of my fragmented memories. What happened is actually a normal process called *dissociation*. I'm sure you've heard of people who are in car accidents and don't remember the actual crash. The brain has a way of protecting you during traumatic events. You basically leave your body and hover somewhere overhead where you can hide, viewing but not feeling what's happening to you. It's nature's way of protecting you. My early years were so painful they stayed locked up in my mind for decades. Then, after working with professionals who deal with hardcore abuse and cults, the details very slowly returned. For some people, buried memories can come back like—wham! All of a sudden you're in this full-blown state of chronic shock. It's like experiencing the trauma all over again; you feel like you're still in it. This is what happens with PTSD.

K. C. Armstrong: Do you think the memories were lost because you were so young and didn't understand that you were being manipulated or why any of these things were happening to you?

Jade McAuliffe: Oh yes. That's exactly what I kept asking my mother: "Why did this and that happen?"

My mom would say, "I don't know. Go ask your father."

"Mom, why did I get a shot in the middle of the night?"

"I don't know. Go ask your father." Who in their right mind responds that way?

K. C. Armstrong: Wait, you would get shots in the middle of the night?

Jade McAuliffe: Yes, absolutely. We were drugged which makes everything all the more fuzzy. I believe to this day that we were not supposed to remember anything. As a child I was very intuitive, and I was also inquisitive. I was always asking questions about what was happening to me because it didn't make sense.

I didn't know any different. The abuse was presented as though it were normal. I didn't know it was strange not to see a doctor when I was sick, for example. My dad took care of us unless something was really wrong and we needed a specialist.

But other things were happening, too. My emotional problems started early, as you might imagine. I had a bag packed when I was five wanting to leave. By the time I was fourteen, I told my mom I needed to talk to somebody because I couldn't handle what was going on. By that time my brother had started abusing me. He had been explosive and violent since age ten, when I was just four. I can forgive my brother though because he too was a victim of this horror, and our father was merciless with him.

K. C. Armstrong: Did your mother participate or have any idea what was happening in this cult?

Jade McAuliffe: I think she had an idea. She claims she doesn't, but that can't be true. But I know, and I'm not supposed to. I started seeking out professionals who dealt with hardcore abuse cases on a quest to figure out the truth. I was looking for healing, but most of all I needed the truth. I had been lied to all the time by my parents, so I was determined to find someone who could explain this to me.

K. C. Armstrong: What went on, and what was the effect on you?

Jade McAuliffe: It was all about fear, judgment and punishment. The pain is extreme: physical, sexual, and emotional. You're always afraid somebody is going to die, that you're going to die. You're not going to make it. You don't tell; you don't talk. If you did, there'd be major consequences. It's like you're broken down to be rebuilt in a different way, if that makes sense.

You end up feeling like you're a monster. You feel like you're the devil walking around because you're the cause of all of this. *Look at what you did.* They take the truth or whatever you did and twist it, making you look like the bad guy.

You did this. You're unworthy and you deserve whatever we're going to give you. You're nothing.

K. C. Armstrong: Oh, my God. Do you have any idea of how big this cult may have been? Do you think there were a lot of people experiencing the same thing as you?

Jade McAuliffe: I'm not sure how big the community was honestly, but I know it was a multi-generational system. From what I understand, my area is a very big hub for cults, but of course they are hidden. There are all different kinds of cults, different sects, different types of religions involved. There are satanic cults. But it wasn't like a commune, where people live in close proximity. In our case, this kind of stuff just happened at night. We'd be taken out of the house someplace after dark. I don't even know where. But I remember telling myself, "I have to ask why I'm getting these shots. I have to ask why."

K. C. Armstrong: With this mind control, torture and manipulation, I can't even imagine the effect on your developing view of the world. What was your general outlook?

Jade McAuliffe: I felt that the world is not a safe place. I didn't want to go outside, but I never really understood why.

K. C. Armstrong: Maybe you were trying to isolate yourself? You never knew what to expect, and you didn't feel safe. Were you very depressed at this point?

Jade McAuliffe: I'm sure I was clinically depressed by the time I was eight. I said that to my dad one time, and he told me I had "no right" to be depressed. Then he walked out of my room, and I thought, "Well, that doesn't change how I feel." By the time I was fourteen, I told my mom I needed help, and she sent me to therapy. But my parents were both very careful about who they sent me to, so I didn't get anywhere. When I was about sixteen we started family therapy where my mother found out about my dad's addiction to violent porn. By that time I had begun feeling suicidal.

We were all in family therapy where my dad even manipulated the therapist. She told me that I should be kinder to my father because he was a very sensitive man. I would shake my head and think, "Oh my God, lady—you have NO IDEA." At this point, I didn't remember any of the really bad stuff, and he wasn't volatile every single day. Abusers don't abuse every day. That's the confusing part. When they're trying to cover up, there are times when they're nice to you. They can even shower gifts on you. They are like Dr. Jekyll and Mr. Hyde; you never know which one you are going to get. It didn't help that my mother was in such denial. She was not a strong person so she would be on our side when we went to her with complaints, but then my dad would come home. She would do an about-face and totally open the floodgates for him to do whatever he wanted. We'd be left feeling completely abandoned.

K. C. Armstrong: Do you think your mother was afraid of the repercussions for going against her husband?

Jade McAuliffe: I don't know. In her defense, I'm not sure she knew everything he did. She knew we were all falling apart and acting out, but she didn't want to believe the accusations of abuse.

K. C. Armstrong: Jade, your childhood was one that no child should ever have to experience. You mentioned acting out, being virtually tortured, abused, lied to, and having very little support. This must have all reached an unbearable intensity at some point.

Jade McAuliffe: It did. As I told you, I began feeling suicidal at sixteen. Then my bulimia morphed into anorexia in my early twenties, and I was hospitalized several times. I had no idea how to care for myself and secretly wished to die. My first suicide attempt occurred at age twenty-eight, and I woke up on a ventilator with a doctor stating sternly in my ear that I'd have to fight hard if I wanted to have the tube removed. I did everything I could to improve and feel better, and my therapy included yet another hospitalization as well as shock treatments.

Almost one year later I attempted suicide again, but I threw up the pills I had swallowed before they could take effect. I was angry, but I knew at that moment that God didn't want me. I remember throwing my hands up and yelling, "Alright! If You want me here, show me what to do!"

K. C. Armstrong: I can't even imagine going through this.

Jade McAuliffe: Generational trauma can destroy families. About six months after my second suicide attempt, I received news that my oldest sister was taken to the hospital because she'd stopped breathing. When the phone rang early the next morning, I knew she was gone. Physically she had been suffering from a second back surgery, and emotionally she was suffering from the childhood we had shared. I watched her disintegrate quickly that year.

K. C. Armstrong: Jade, I know there's even more to this shocking story.

Jade McAuliffe: Yes. I had such a hard time with my oldest sister's death, but at least my middle sister and I had each other to get through it together. At that time she and I were disconnected from the other members of our family. Sometimes people are toxic. In order for you to get better, you may have to cut ties or go silent with members of your own family to move forward.

That's what my middle sister and I had to do. Luckily we had each other, but around 2008 my middle sister started struggling with depression. Before that she had problems with anxiety, but I had been the one that was dealing with depression, in and out of hospitals. She had never been in a hospital, wasn't on any medication, and always seemed to me to handle everything so well. She had graduated from college, but after losing her job she was having trouble finding another one. I think when you come from a dysfunctional family where you're traumatized, it really takes a toll on you eventually.

I'd been working on my depression for decades, and she'd worked on hers for a while, but I think she stopped. Once she started going downhill, she went down fast. She had always been more than my sister; she was my surrogate mother, my mentor and my advocate. She was the go-to in the family for, "Here's my problem. How would you solve it?"

> *I was determined not to become another statistic. Everything changed as I stepped into my power.*

She was very steady and when she didn't make it, I thought, "Oh my God. I might not make it either. How am I going to do this without my sister?" She had always been there for me, even when we weren't close geographically. She was my strength. She was one of the only people that ever stood up for me in my lifetime. She even stood up to my parents on my behalf.

Minutes after finding out she was dead, I had an urge to really harm myself. I just wanted to be with her. It scared me. I thought, "I have to get myself some help."

The moment I made that decision to go on, everything changed. I woke up and claimed my space in the world. I stopped putting my needs on the back burner and started taking care of myself for the very first time. I was forty-eight and completely shattered, but I was determined not to become another statistic. Everything changed as I stepped into my power.

I started trying alternatives to talk therapy (energy work), and my healing accelerated. I learned how to ground myself and live in my body again. I started accepting all of my parts including the "dark" ones. I stopped looking for validation outside myself and learned to self-soothe. I felt safer and less anxious.

By listening intently to my own inner voice, I began healing from the inside and for the very first time was finally living in a whole-hearted way. On my quest for self-love and acceptance, I discovered life coaching and began investing in my own well-being and success.

K. C. Armstrong: And here is where you applied that change within to help others cope with their suffering as suicide loss survivors. This is so amazing and explains why your book which helps survivors of suicide loss became an instant bestseller. It is clearly written from the heart, and people who are most in need of your wisdom can recognize that authenticity immediately, I'm sure. Tell us now about your intentions for your book.

Jade McAuliffe: I've taken all of the personal trauma and heartache that I've been telling you about and used it to create a sort of guide book. I wanted to do this partly because of the stigma still surrounding suicide; so many people end up grieving alone or silently because they have no place to turn where people will help them. As a whole, people feel like they're carrying some sort of disease when they're going through this because other people are afraid to approach them. People don't know what to say, and as a result many avoid us when we need them the most.

There's such a heaviness that goes along with suicide grief and, while it makes a lot of people uncomfortable, it makes those going through it feel really isolated. I wanted to create a book that would gently take suicide loss survivors by the hand and love them through their experience. Certainly grief is not one-size-fits-all, and it takes a considerable amount of time to understand your own. But I hope this book can be a helpful part of the process.

K. C. Armstrong: That has to be such a great comfort to anyone going through such a painful time in their lives. I'm sure survivors feel that no one understands, and they're probably right. I can't imagine how carrying on one's life after losing a loved one in this way feels. To hear from someone who has experienced both sides—as a loss survivor and suicide attempt survivor—readers can feel confident that someone else may understand some of what they're going through. This can ease that isolation you were just talking about. I believe you do one-on-one coaching as well?

Jade McAuliffe: Yes. Through my book and life coaching I want to give people permission to grieve in their own way and time, but with some practical tips and tools. When you lose someone to suicide, you feel like the rug has come out from underneath your life. Suddenly, you don't know who you are, what you're supposed to do, how to feel. You're confused and angry, with so many intense emotions pulling you in every direction. You tend to isolate yourself, but at the same time you want people to support you. They don't know what to say, and you don't know what you want to hear. It's all confusing and absolutely devastating.

Through *Wake Me From the Nightmare* I want to share methods that really helped me create a safe space to grieve and empower myself. The idea is to give people a useful guide that can meet them right where they are. The book is written like a love letter.

K. C. Armstrong: What is a good way that someone who is listening or reading right now can get themselves out of that dark place if they are depressed, doubting their ability to function, or thinking about hurting themselves? You told me last time that people at greater risk of attempting suicide are suicide loss survivors, especially first degree family members, which I find shocking.

Jade McAuliffe: Right. First, I want suicide loss survivors to know there is no validity in the thought that "I shouldn't be feeling this way. There's something wrong with me." I'm going to tell you right now, there is nothing wrong with you. You are not to blame. If you're depressed, there's a reason for that. There's a reason for every single feeling that we have. And when we can surrender to those feelings and let them be without judging them, then they can move through us. We will eventually feel relief. Healing is cyclical, not linear. When you're down, you will come back up again; the downs don't last forever. But if you've been down for too long, definitely find some help. At the very least, you can always call the suicide prevention lifeline (800-273-8255).

Reaching out for support is a really good thing. There are coaches out there that can give you tools to handle the stress if therapy isn't the best fit. We all need someone to witness our journeys and our feelings. None of us have to do this healing thing alone.

K. C. Armstrong: Through your long journey toward your new understanding, what would you like to add at this point in your story?

Jade McAuliffe: For one thing, I no longer view the world as a scary place. I've come to learn it will be whatever I make of it. My experiences have taught me to respect all people, their stories, and the fragility of life. For the very first time in my life, I embrace my entire story and am sharing it with others.

I have been so blessed to witness through my children the healing power of love. They have given me purpose and keep me focused on moving forward and breaking the generational darkness of our lineage. I know, in my soul, the work I continue to do on myself will heal my kids, my estranged family, and future generations. I love my family. All of them. I understand that hurting people hurt people. I'm doing this for all of us.

In 2016, I joined the Walworth County Suicide Prevention Education and Awareness Coalition and, in 2017 and 2018, I co-chaired the Walworth County Out of the Darkness Community Walk for suicide awareness and prevention.

I currently volunteer for the American Foundation for Suicide Prevention's Healing Conversations Program (formerly known as the Survivor Outreach Program), which offers personal support to survivors of suicide loss, and I offer one-on-one coaching sessions on my website *NoParameters.org*.

Today my passions are postvention and teaching others how to create and sustain genuine and meaningful connections. In short, I help suicide loss survivors feel like themselves again, and I intend to make a difference in the lives of others touched by trauma, grief, and suicide loss.

Most of all, I want others to know that life can get better and that you don't have to keep searching for someone else to save you. All you have to do is look within and listen closely to your body. Everything you need resides right there. You don't have to do this alone.

K. C. Armstrong: Thank you, Jade, for telling us your story and how you were able to reach a place of forgiveness and compassion for others. I can see that all this work you are doing can uplift so many people and also affirm your new, positive outlook on life. This is why we at WMAP have a special place of admiration for you as one of the *World's Most Amazing Women*.

More information about Jade:

Website: http://www.noparameters.org.
Book: *Wake Me from the Nightmare: Hope, Healing, and Empowerment After Suicide Loss*

RE-INVENTION

an interview with Danielle Shay

Danielle Shay seemed to live an idyllic life until the illusion faded and she wisely re-invented herself as a devoted mother, successful market analyst, trader, and financial commentator

INTRODUCTION:

Danielle Shay believes that there is an opportunity everywhere, and if you decide to go for something you don't quit. Danielle does not sit at the side of the pool and put her pinky toe in the shallow end to see if the water is warm. She's more the type to run straight to the high dive to make the biggest splash. If you see someone that has her determination, get ready, or get out of the pool.

Danielle exemplifies that it's never too late to start fresh, even when it doesn't seem that you can. She protected herself and her son by taking the initiative to flee abuse and make a safe life through a totally new career field. Danielle shows you how to embrace the experiences you have in life and work through them. Even when you find yourself in a place you never imagined, you really can figure it out and create your best life.

INTERVIEW:

K. C. Armstrong: Our next guest seemed to live a Utopian life, at least for a while. But, sadly, her vision of the future was interrupted by deceit, disappointment, and even poverty. Welcome, Danielle Shay. We love stories of victories like yours. You were thrown a curve in your life and had opportunities to give in or give up; instead, you had the drive to keep moving forward to recreate yourself. I can't wait to share your story, but first, how are you today?

Danielle Shay: I'm great K. C.

K. C. Armstrong: Glad to hear that. Danielle, tell us about the young idealist who moved to Central America to prepare for the Peace Corp.

Danielle Shay: Sure, K.C. Throughout college I studied international law and human rights, and I went to Costa Rica because I wanted to do some volunteer work in preparation for volunteering for the Peace Corps. I figured I'd work on my Spanish and teach elementary students in Costa Rica to gain some experience. I taught English, Math, and Science to sixth graders and thought eventually I'd return to the States and go to law school. I lived on the beach in Costa Rica for three years, and while I was there, I fell in love. My life was great, even though I didn't make a lot of money. At the time, it didn't really matter.

K. C. Armstrong: You were living an adventure in Costa Rica—gorgeous surroundings, good job, and a fiancé you loved. What could possibly go wrong?

Danielle Shay: It didn't work out how I had planned. In the beginning, everything was great. Everything was amazing. That's why I got engaged and wanted to have a child to begin with. My biggest mistake has always been trusting people too much, and I was duped. I thought my fiancé was a responsible business owner, but things weren't at all as they seemed. We were together for three years, but it wasn't until I was pregnant that he became abusive and the truth came out about his life. I heard that's how it usually happens with abusers—they turn on the charm and rope you in until they have you; however, it was quite shocking to me.

At this point, I was making a very low salary, $545 per month, because I had left my higher paying job managing a restaurant for a more "suitable" job with a better schedule to raise my son. The hours were better and I had health insurance, but I depended on my fiancé to pay for our house and car since I was making the lower salary of the two of us. This is where the trouble began because I was financially trapped with him after he became controlling.

K. C. Armstrong: It's amazing, isn't it, that you think you really know someone in a relationship, and all of a sudden you see a whole different side?

Danielle Shay: It is crazy. Once I became pregnant, he let me know that I was his possession. I had to do everything he said, and when I didn't comply, he showed me who was the boss. He thought he could treat me however he wanted because I didn't have anywhere else to go, and I was going to have his child. He was selfish and basically used me as an incubator. One example is how we previously had once a week sushi dates; however, pregnant women aren't supposed to eat sushi, and being around it made me feel really nauseous (and

I love sushi!). This was my doctor's advice, plus it made me sick. Up until then we had gone on weekly sushi dates, but that wouldn't be possible for a while. He told me he didn't care how I felt, he was still getting his sushi—that I was the pregnant one, not him. And that's what he did, taking our car, and leaving me at home. This wasn't just once. It was multiple times per week, for months on end.

He would go out with other women, too. Very quickly he was spending six nights a week at the bar, taking our car, my money out of our safe, and leaving me trapped alone at home. This was before the days of Uber. He made sure to take any cash I had in the house when he would leave, so I couldn't get a taxi. I did that once, and he made sure it didn't happen again. He would hang out in the bars until three or four am. If I got upset, he'd get violent. While he was doing all this, I didn't have anyone to lean on, except coworkers, because he wouldn't allow me to go anywhere other than home and school, and he would time me to be sure I didn't make any stops. I dropped my girlfriend off after school one day, making me ten minutes late to get home (he timed me), and he never let me use the car again. I was too embarrassed to tell my family.

I could never imagine that happening, and I don't know why it happens. This was just so far outside my experience that I never saw it coming. The days of romantic vacations, frequent dates, and little gifts were long gone. When I complained about how he treated me, he got mean and violent. Once his violence came out, I knew it was no longer safe, for me, my son, or my dogs. I went through eight months of pregnancy living like this, and it caused me an incredible amount of stress—and I began planning my escape.

K. C. Armstrong: Do you think the idea of becoming a father terrified your fiancé and caused this change? Had you talked about the possibility of children?

Danielle Shay: Actually, we had. He begged to have a child. I knew we would have to change our free-spirited lifestyle to settle down and have a child. That was something we both were excited about. My ex had always promised me that once we were married, we'd live a beautiful, traditional family life. But once I became pregnant, he transformed into a whole different person.

It was crazy—but I hoped he would change when he saw his son. Before this happened, I would wonder sometimes how women could become single mothers. How are things so bad that you're willing to leave the father of your baby? Of course, that was just hypothetical. Now, I know what it's like for things to be so bad that yes, you are willing to leave your house and everything you own and start over.

K. C. Armstrong: So, you were trapped—pregnant, too scared to tell your family, and financially dependent on an abuser. What did you do?

Danielle Shay: I left my fiancé. I had a newborn, two suitcases, about eight hundred dollars, and nowhere to go but back home with my parents in the States. Since I had to leave my job when I left him, I didn't have health insurance. Two weeks before my baby was born, I had to apply for Medicaid, which was an extreme low point in my life.

K. C. Armstrong: It must have been awful.

Danielle Shay: It was the worst time of my life. I was lonely and scared, and I didn't know where to turn. When I was in Costa Rica, I was in another country far from my family. I wasn't a citizen and couldn't attain citizenship until after my son was born or until after we got married, so my ability to own property was limited. I knew I could no longer marry my fiancé because it wasn't safe for me and my son, so I had to figure out how to escape and support us. I was homeless without him, because my fiancé had put the house and our car in his name. He told me with our "common law" marriage, I was entitled to half of what we built together. That never happened.

63

K. C. Armstrong: When you guys first got together you could never see this coming. But, all of a sudden, you had big decisions to make.

Danielle Shay: Yes, that's right. While I was In Costa Rica, my father told me, "You're never going to be able to survive making this type of money, and you know you need to do something to expand your earning power and take care of yourself." He also said, "I don't want you to ever depend on a husband to support you in life. You have to take care of yourself because you never know what's going to happen." I kept telling him I was fine, but of course I finally understood exactly what he meant. My dad was always there to encourage me, but I didn't tell him the full story until things got bad.

K. C. Armstrong: It's great that your father was always there to advise you. Were you guys always so tight?

Danielle Shay: Yes, but we became even closer through this experience. Growing up, I wasn't too much of a rule-follower or person to follow blindly. But he really backed me up when I needed it. Seeing my situation, he said, "Why don't you consider a different career? Why don't you consider trading stock options? This would give you the ability to make money from home, so you wouldn't have to put your son into daycare. Plus, you'll have more earning potential than what you have as a teacher."

K. C. Armstrong: Most teachers don't make that kind of drastic move, but you had experience communicating and clarifying challenging concepts, right?

Danielle Shay: Yes. I was an elementary teacher and coach for years. I taught self-esteem courses for girls and taught English as a second language for adults. I've been trained at breaking concepts down. You know what teachers do, right? They introduce a topic, break it down into steps, and give you supplementary study materials. Then they give you quizzes to make sure that you know what you're doing and find out any weak spots. These are the skills that I applied to trading and teaching trading.

K. C. Armstrong: Did you realize that you had the tools to become so successful in trading?

Danielle Shay: At the time? I had absolutely no idea!

K. C. Armstrong: But I bet your dad told you that you would be good at this, right?

Danielle Shay: Not really! He hoped this would work out, and so did I.

K. C. Armstrong: They say everything happens for a reason. Another way of saying that might be that skills and education are never lost because you can reinvent yourself using tools you've picked up walking down other paths. So your teaching talents helped you establish yourself in your new career.

It's a real skill to explain something so complex to someone like myself who is baffled by the subject. Did you always have such confidence? Even after the betrayal you went through, you obviously felt you could handle something completely outside your comfort zone.

Danielle Shay: Actually, I had zero confidence. The first nine months that I was trying to learn how to trade had nothing to do with believing in myself. It was just that I had no other choice. It's funny, because people say to me, "How did you go from not knowing anything about the market to becoming a guest contributor on major TV networks?" My answer is simple: I had no other option. My back was against the wall. I was determined to do something so I didn't have to put my son in daycare. You know, I was scared. I was by myself. But my parents were amazing. They pretty much raised Leo with me until I married my amazing husband. Right after the baby was born, I had tried to work a couple of different jobs in photography and waitressing, and it was terrible. I worked long hours and had to leave Leo all day long in daycare, which was expensive. I was determined to trade and to be good at it. After a while I gained confidence. But there was definitely very little in the beginning.

K. C. Armstrong: I love the fact that you just said, "I had no other option. I had to get good at this." Did that attitude and determination all come from your father, or did you have other positive influences in your life?

Danielle Shay: My mother and my grandmother are both very strong women from a large Catholic family. In the Catholic religion, being an unwed mother is one of the most shameful things that you can bestow upon your whole family. I remember talking to my grandmother when I was trying to decide if I should leave my fiancé or not. I told her how terrible he was to me and how I worried that everyone would be ashamed of me if I didn't marry him. My ninety-year-old, devout-and wise-grandmother told me I should not bear with abuse. She told me I should stop caring what anyone else thinks and do what's best for me and my son. She said it's better to be unmarried than to be married to someone that mistreats me.

K. C. Armstrong: That's not what you were expecting!

Danielle Shay: No, but it was a tremendous comfort. And my mother echoed that opinion as well. My mother, grandmother, and my dad let me know that they certainly never expected me, a graduate from one of the best colleges in the state, to become a single mother. However, they were unified in the belief that it would be better to be a single mother than to be married to someone who controls you.

K. C. Armstrong: Totally. I mean, that is the coolest thing that your grandmother was able to show you in that way how much she loves you and cares about your happiness.

Danielle Shay: When someone you love is in a jam, I think everything else goes out the window, and you just care about their well-being.

K. C. Armstrong: I agree. What people think isn't important. So, you learned how to trade options and eventually to teach the process to others. How long have you been doing this now?

Danielle Shay: I've been trading since 2013. I trade options rather than stocks because you can do so with a small account, which is what I had when I first started.

K. C. Armstrong: That's different from what I was imagining; I figured that you need a sizable bank account to even think about trading.

Danielle Shay: That's a common thought. But what you can do is start with a small sum and continually add to it. In options, you can start with around $5,000 and trade small quantities. In my job as an educator, I teach people to do this starting on a small scale, if that's what they want. When I first started, I traded $200 at a time.

K. C. Armstrong: What is actually involved?

Danielle Shay: I buy and hold stocks as an investor, but I also trade options on a short-term basis. I use a top down process when analyzing the stock market to identify high probability trades and investing ideas. I start with the major indexes: The S&P, the Dow, and the Nasdaq. Then, I select the best performing index and identify stocks within the index that are strong as well. For example, Microsoft is a ticker that fits these criteria. An *investor* would just buy Microsoft stock and hold it forever, right? But as an *options trader,* I can enter a trade for a couple days or a few weeks, with a smaller dollar amount at risk due to the leverage of options, without staying in the stock for the long term.

K. C. Armstrong: That's pretty cool!

Danielle Shay: I had never heard of it until my father explained it to me. Options are just a little bit different from what most people know because they're more leveraged than stock, and they also have a time value. What that means is that they expire after a certain amount of time. You're placing a trade with the assumption Microsoft (for example) will go up within the next month. The question is, "How can I trade that in a leveraged way that'll allow me to make more money than if I just bought the stock alone?" For someone like myself with a small account, it makes a lot of sense.

K. C. Armstrong: It sounds like you've absorbed a tremendous amount of strategy and information since leaving your teaching position.

Danielle Shay: That is the craziest part about all of it. I learned from the educational trading company that I now work for, *Simpler Trading.* My second round of university was going through the different classes that my mentor was offering at the time. They have a live trading room, which is where I would listen online while taking care of my son. Then, I'd take classes on the weekends. Studying full time is how I became proficient.

It's definitely not a quick or easy journey. I think for the first year and a half I was still pretty green, not really understanding what I was doing. It took me about three years before I felt competent enough to teach. That, of course, was why my mentor initially hired me; he had been trading for thirty years, and he wanted someone that could speak to new traders.

I honestly think that my studies in this area were more valuable than my university education. The amount of time and money that I've spent on trading has been far more beneficial to me than what I spent on my university degree. It opened up a whole range of possibilities because I can trade from anywhere and have a job in a higher paying industry.

K. C. Armstrong: Danielle, what is one piece of advice that you would give somebody starting to trade stocks?

Danielle Shay: I think the most important thing to know is that on a historical basis, the market goes up over the span of a person's lifetime. The stock market is higher than it was twenty years ago. You hear in the news, "Oh no, the market's

> *everybody has to start somewhere, so it might as well be you, today*

down. Sell this and that." But if you think about it as long-term savings, that downturn is the easiest way to get in—when prices are low. I trade options on a short-term basis which is a little bit more complicated, but I also buy and hold stocks for the long run.

K. C. Armstrong: How do people react when they begin working with you? Are they nervous about putting their hard-earned savings at risk?

Danielle Shay: Many people think, "Oh, the stock market is so complicated." I understand because I felt that way too. I remember looking at the charts and thinking, "Oh my gosh, I'm never going to be able to read that." But John, my mentor, taught me to look for a pattern, something that is happening over and over again. First, you have to let people teach you. They say, "Hey, this is a pattern I've seen, and this is how you find and trade it." Then, if you stick with it, you get better and find your own patterns. I just took it one step at a time.

K. C. Armstrong: It must have been hard to stay positive when you thought the world was crashing around you and everything was a daily struggle. What got you through? I'm sure many people would have folded.

Danielle Shay: Well, in the beginning I felt like, oh it's going to take so long! But I forged ahead. I really like the quote, "The expert in anything was once a beginner." If you think of it that way, everybody has to start somewhere, so it might as well be you, today. This helped when I felt discouraged.

But most of all, the motivation was my son. The thing is, most people don't understand what it's like to raise a child alone—to be the one responsible for his safety, health, and happiness. People say, "How can that happen? How do you end up as a single mom or a single dad?" Well, misfortune happens all the time. You know, you can get into a relationship and find out that your partner's abusive. You can find out that they're cheating on you, or they're stealing from you, or so many other possibilities. There are a lot of single parents out there, and I think there's still a stigma surrounding parenting alone. But what I have found is that my son was my reason to do everything that I did, and he was what gave me the inspiration to work for a better life for us both. I knew that *me alone* was better than *me together* with his biological father. And I knew I had to make it work.

K. C. Armstrong: Once you have a child, his needs fill your world, right?

Danielle Shay: Yes, of course.

K. C. Armstrong: By the way, I love the quote about every expert starting at one time as a beginner. Sometimes you just have to take a leap, and I think that's something that most single parents, most people generally, need to realize. Even though your dream may not come this year, it will come at last. The years will pass anyway.

There are people who feel that the world is coming down on them, and they're not where they thought they would be at a particular time in their life. It could be a relationship, a job, or something else that doesn't work out the way they hope. Even if that's a common feeling, it's still a hard thing to go through. Do you think your troubles made you the success that you are today? I know you always had a great work ethic, but as hard as you worked, the unexpected still happened.

Danielle Shay: Oh, it definitely has. Having the right mentor and positive people around me encouraged me, and they were important to my success. You have to watch out for the "soul suckers," who bring you down by saying *you can't* or *it's too hard* or *it'll never happen*. I try to focus on positive people and energies. You want to water the flowers and not the weeds, right?

K. C. Armstrong: Great way to say it! And is that the positive attitude that brought the man of your dreams, now your husband, into your life?

Danielle Shay: Oh definitely. When we met, he said he loved my absolute refusal to give up. At that time, I hadn't yet decided that I was going to be a trader. But I had decided I was going to be successful.

From the beginning he told me, "Whatever you want, whatever you think, I'll support you." Having people like that are in your corner is so important. There were days when I never thought I would get out of the rut, but then small successes started to happen. I appreciated and tried to get more of them, and things improved.

K. C. Armstrong: It's a beautiful thing to have someone believe in you so strongly. Danielle, you are obviously the type of person who does not like to be told *you can't* or *you won't*. You may even thrive on proving those doubters wrong.

Danielle Shay: True. It gives me a lot of strength.

K. C. Armstrong: Thinking back, isn't it strange how good things can grow out of bad? Do you think your challenges made a path for something better to come into your life?

Danielle Shay: Well, I know I never would have tried to master trading options if I wasn't in a spot where I had to figure out a career that would support me and my son. But it was the best thing that has ever happened to me. Yes, it was painful having a newborn alone and dealing with someone like my ex-fiancé, and it was really terrible for at least three years while I was trying to catch my footing in the financial world. However, now I speak at conferences all the time and have hundreds of members that I get to teach every day. I never would be here if it weren't for the hardship I went through, and I am so grateful for that. So yes, I'd say it's because of the painful ordeal I went through that I'm in such a great place today. Another result of my experiences is that I've learned to stand up for myself. I will never allow myself, or my son, to be treated badly. I don't give second chances, and I protect my son with all I have.

K. C. Armstrong: Not a bad lesson to learn. Sometimes we give too much of ourselves and wind up being taken advantage of. Your story began that way, but you gained wisdom as you went along and had to rethink your life and your choices. And now you are not only stronger for yourself, but you are also able to make a positive impact on people around you.

Danielle Shay: You know, K. C., I have always loved helping people, maybe because I am the oldest in a large family and am very close with my siblings. Today I have a beautiful family, and I get to help people every single day. I inspire others to seek out financial freedom—just like I did. My story was that I was a single mom. Others want control of their finances and their financial future for any number of reasons. I can help them along on this journey.

K. C. Armstrong: Any words of advice for someone who is struggling to find his or her own place in the world? Perhaps something you could tell someone who needs to change direction and recover from a situation something like yours?

Danielle Shay: When you're going through hell, keep going. If you stop, you give in to the situation so just keep moving forward until you see where you belong. Remember, the years will still pass. Do you want to be in the same place you are now, or will you have made the sacrifices necessary to find yourself in a place you really want to be?

K. C. Armstrong: Thanks, Danielle. We always appreciate encouragement to try new things and reinvent ourselves when necessary. It's always a pleasure to hear from you because you are a great example of staying positive and making things happen instead of waiting for chance to put you in a better situation. For this and more, we thank you for being a *Simply Amazing Woman*!

More information about Danielle:

Website: www.simplertrading.com/women
Twitter: @traderDanielle
Instagram: traderdanielleshay618

SOUL TRAVELER

an interview with Marilynn Hughes

Marilynn Hughes tells of visions and out of body travel in her personal, spiritual quest and is involved in non-denominational charitable projects around the world

INTRODUCTION:

Who is to say what ideas and beliefs are better or more valid than others? I think that when we are closed-minded we miss out on amazing possibilities. Marilynn Hughes' message is unique, and if we open our hearts and minds, we can see how she helps others with her special gifts and knowledge.

I find the detail in this chapter both fascinating and exciting. I'm going to ask you to suspend your disbelief for the time it takes to read and digest the whole interview. There is so much we don't know about the universe. I'm not asking you to agree with everything in this chapter, or in this book for that matter, but I do hope you'll consider some new possibilities. For those who have experienced or simply believe in Marilynn's topic of *Out of Body Travel*, I'm sure you'll be amazed!

INTERVIEW:

K. C. Armstrong: You guys are going to be knocked out by my next guest because her topic is one you don't hear about every day. This is something I find so interesting, and I hope you do, too. Marilynn Hughes is the founder of the *Out of Body Travel Foundation*, has written more than ninety-eight books, produced multiple magazine articles and CD's, and has had literally thousands of out of body experiences herself. All of her online resources are available for free download, and she is involved in charitable projects around the world. Welcome, Marilynn. I can't wait for our audience to hear your story.

Marilynn Hughes: Oh, thank you for having me. I'm looking forward to sharing my experiences with you.

K. C. Armstrong: Marilynn, I see on your website that you founded the *Out of Body Travel Foundation* in 2003 and that your stated mission is "to reduce spiritual and physical hunger worldwide." That's quite an aspiration, and I can't wait to hear how it came about and the process of working toward that goal. What was your early life like, Marilynn?

Marilynn Hughes: I was born in Glendora, California, to a German mother and a scientist father. They met when he was studying overseas in Freiburg, Germany, for his doctorate in mathematics. I had one older brother and one sister. My mother was able to leave Germany literally the same year the Berlin Wall went up, 1962. My father worked on a lot of things during his lifetime: the development of rocket science, radar, and the beginnings of artificial intelligence. I have three adult children, two daughters and a son. I've had more than my share of adversity, including rape, family alienation, religious persecution, illness, and near death; nevertheless, today I live a blessed life as a mystic, writer and spiritual counselor.

K. C. Armstrong: It's hard to know where to begin! But you told me earlier that at the age of nine years old, you had a life-changing epiphany which you must describe for us.

Marilynn Hughes: Yes, K. C. At age nine the Lord presented to me the very clear vision of a cross on fire, and I was trying to put it out. In this vision, certain people in the world could only see the fire, not the cross. Every time I put the fire out, they would relight the flame to the cross. Battling our fundamental differences seemed to continue without end, but finally, due to the grace of God, I was able to put the fire out completely, allowing the cross to stand tall.

Then the Lord spoke to me: "The fire represents ignorance, and the cross, awareness." He conveyed that there would be much fire in my life, but that I would bear the cross. Many people would never see it, and this would cause frustration. "At a future time, you will take that cross to the world and present it as a living vision of the reality of God. Though others may think you are foolish, you are special."

K. C. Armstrong: I'm speechless! All the time you were trying to put out the fire of ignorance, people would feed it—keep it going. After what seemed a very long time, you were able to put out the fire and allow awareness to "stand tall." Unbelievable! And you were told that some would think you "foolish." Is this the case?

Marilynn Hughes: Perhaps. But I have to tell you, in that vision the Lord filled my spirit with a love I can not describe.

K. C. Armstrong: Marilynn, we'll be talking a lot about "out of body experience." What IS that?

Marilynn Hughes: An out of body travel experience (OBTE) happens when your spirit separates from your physical body. It's similar to a near-death experience. The spirit separates from the physical body and travels in the overlapping and parallel spheres that comprise our universe. We are incarnate on this earth for a very short period of time and for a very specific purpose. If we don't use our time well, according to the purpose for which we have been brought here, we literally are just standing still. There is a purification journey that we are meant to undertake.

We live in what are called the *mortal realms*, where the battles between good and evil take place both within ourselves and also outside of us. We experience internal struggles of choice and external battles such as war and violence. Does that make sense?

K. C. Armstrong: I'm following you.

Marilynn Hughes: Generally, we have been brought here to become aware of incorrect understandings relating to the nature of eternal love or eternal purpose. This is where delusion is coming from. These are karmic issues that arise from vice, from sin, or in the Buddhist tradition from fetters or cravings—things that people are attached to that hold them back from moving forward or closer to God. If a soul does not push itself forward in the purification process, it can actually go backwards. Think of a spacecraft and how it has to shift into gear before it can take off. We must do that as souls; we have to get into the proper gear before we can take off.

K. C. Armstrong: What do these out of body experiences feel like?

Marilynn Hughes: When you first have these experiences, you may very well be earthbound; you may see your body from above your bed. You may be floating around a room or even floating around the Earth. But the purpose of out of body travel is not to remain in those earthbound states. When you go through the experience fully, you will be traveling to the heavens, the hells, and the purgatories. There is a multiplicity in the universe, an infinite number of interplanetary worlds. There are the galactic heavens and infinite heavenly realms that are just impossible to describe. But that's where we're looking to go. And as the soul moves in that direction, a true journey of purification can begin and the soul can actually start moving ahead.

K. C. Armstrong: Marilynn, you have used this gift to improve the spirituality of yourself and others, but it seems to be a mixed blessing. You were told at nine that you would have much "fire" in your life as well as frustration in your journey. Did you ever think of not pursuing your ability to interact with the other worlds around us?

Marilynn Hughes: Once I started having these experiences regularly, it became a clear calling from within me that I could not ignore. I would literally be instructed as to every step along the way—what I needed to do next. Whenever I was tempted to ignore it, it was like getting pounded from within. I would hear this strong voice: *far greater significance…far greater significance…* It was like God would not let it be. It was an undeniable calling that I had to fulfill, or I would have no peace. So I began the *Out of Body Travel Foundation* in 2003. It was founded partly on the words of Mother Teresa who said that the spiritual poverty of the West was even more serious and severe than the physical poverty she'd experienced in other parts of the world. I made the decision to reduce spiritual hunger worldwide, and we started out by making spiritual information freely downloadable, available worldwide from our Foundation website.

K. C. Armstrong: Let's talk some more about this out of body travel, OK? It's so interesting but unfamiliar and a little strange to most of us.

Marilynn Hughes: Sure. When I started having these experiences early on, I started journaling them, and I've been writing books about them ever since.

K. C. Armstrong: Obviously these experiences had a profound effect on your life, and you spent lots of time writing about them. But why a foundation? How did that come about?

Marilynn Hughes: Ironically, it was my first publisher who suggested that we start the O*ut of Body Travel Foundation* so I have to give him credit for the idea. I was having these spontaneous experiences at the time. I had done some reading on pioneers in the field, like Robert Monroe, and was honored to meet Dr. Raymond Moody, known for actually coining the term "near-death experience" in 1975. But these experiences took me on a spiritual journey inward that went well beyond what I was able to find in the prevailing literature.

As I was journaling heavily on these things, I was inspired to also start compiling the ancient sacred texts from different world religions and traditions that have been written by mystics, sages and prophets through-out history. Many of these early mystics had similar experiences but left their secrets buried in these writings. Gathering them became a real labor of love and a real important journey for me.

K. C. Armstrong: That's intriguing about uncovering forgotten ancient texts. Were you able to gather many?

Marilynn Hughes: I have maybe five thousand of them in my house. But I've been shown this staircase of ancient texts going from earth to heaven, and I'd like you to envision every single one of those steps being one of those sacred texts. Even though many of them are forgotten, all of them left behind the keys—the secrets that their authors learned before transcending to the next realm because they had figured it out. Just consider, for instance, my five thousand texts; every single one presents a different angle from which to view God.

K. C. Armstrong: Do the texts follow the same general principles, or are they very different?

Marilynn Hughes: Looking through them, there is definitely a pattern that has been laid out for us for many thousands of years by the masters. By studying these texts, we are giving ourselves the opportunity to get to know God better. We're looking at Him through different eyes and through different vantage points. How do we approach somebody when we want to be their friend? We get to know them. We have to do the same thing with God. A lot of what I teach people to do involves prayer and a lot of meditation, solitude, and spiritual reading. This is the same as it's been throughout the ages. Looking at these ancient texts, the masters from all the ages have done these very same things, because they work.

K. C. Armstrong: You mentioned meditation. More and more people today seem to be involved in that. Is meditation a part of out of body travel experience?

Marilynn Hughes: Out of body experience is very different from meditation, but meditation is a big part of bringing it about. The difference between meditation and out of body travel is huge. While OBTE is the literal separation of the spirit from your body, meditation is more of a psychic experience; you might even have a visualization when you're meditating, but you are experiencing it on a much less heightened base. I do a lot of meditation and I love it, but it's very different from an out of body experience.

K. C. Armstrong: Marilynn, we talked about several of your life experiences that led to your research, writing and creation of your foundation, notably that first beautiful out of body experience at age nine. You also told us about several intense personal tragedies, including a dire health prognosis as a young mother. Would you tell us more about that?

Marilynn Hughes: Yes. In 2001 I was diagnosed with what appeared to be a terminal condition. Then in 2003, I had a pretty mind-bending near-death experience, which literally changed everything and led to the launch of our Foundation.

K. C. Armstrong: What happened?

Marilynn Hughes: In 2001, I was diagnosed with the combination of cardiomyopathy and heart failure, the most common cause of the need for a heart transplant. I had a moderate to severe case, and at first it seemed like I might do okay on medications. But then I started sinking. So in 2003, after several echocardiograms, we had to consider the possibility of either a heart transplant or another treatment. I spent the night before a decision was to be made on which procedure would be done in the hospital. During the night I went into some arrhythmia. I left my body and started going towards what I call *the heavens*. And there was this beautiful tunnel. One of the things that I'd already learned was once you get to the end of that tunnel, you don't want to touch the veil before you because then you can't go back.

I saw a little black and white dog from my childhood waiting for me in the light. Wow. I didn't have a lot of relatives who had crossed over yet, but my little dog was there waiting for me. At that point, Christ came and took me on a journey through the heavens. It's impossible to describe, but I'll try. It was so incredibly beautiful! The vibrant colors, the variety of hues, flying at the speed of light through all these worlds...

K. C. Armstrong: So hard to imagine!

Marilynnn Hughes: I knew that I'd been given grace because you normally can't do this unless you've made the decision that you're not going back to the earthly realm. I had gone on this fantastic, spectacular journey, but I had three young children at the time. Jesus returned me to a space where I could see my family. With them still in my view, Jesus showed me something truly amazing.

For lack of a better word, it was like a meter which shows our progress in life. Jesus told me that the purpose of earthly life is to go from selfishness to selflessness. He said that I'd accomplished what I needed to and that I could go back to the heavens if I wanted. He showed me the rest of the world and how it would remain a selfish place whether I went back or not.

K. C. Armstrong: I want to pause real quick, before you continue. I want to imagine what you saw. You're going through all these different galaxies. What are you seeing? What are you feeling?

Marilynnn Hughes: It's a world of color-the purples, pinks, blues, whites; you're literally flying through it. There's this ecstatic joy because there's a vibration that is so beautiful and so beyond what we experience in this earthly world. It's so hard to explain. It's just so… once you're there, you definitely do not want to leave, that's for sure. You've probably heard that from people who've had near death experiences; you don't want to leave such beauty and peace.

K. C. Armstrong: Is that heaven, would you say?

Marilynnn Hughes: I would. I was seeing many heavens and many worlds. And there are an infinite number of purgatories and lower realms, too. It's not just one place. It's multidimensional. Many worlds in one world.

K. C. Armstrong: In your work, do you see common patterns in these near-death experiences?

Marilynnn Hughes: Yes, I do. People often see dead relatives. A lot of them will see the tunnel and many will have their life flash before their eyes, so there is a series of things that are generally seen. One of the most common characteristics in legitimate near-death experiences is that people's lives change dramatically when they return. They talk about the way they experienced the unconditional love of God and the universe. They come back with a new, defined purpose, literally becoming different people. Their whole life and purpose change to love and caring and the desire to serve.

K. C. Armstrong: Now, do you think that's because they came in contact with a higher being, or do you think it's maybe because when they come back to this life, they just cherish it a lot more and finally see the beauty in things that they used to take for granted?

Marilynnn Hughes: That's a great question! I would say, from my own experience, it's more the first than the second reason. But it's definitely both because one of the common footprints of a near death experience is that people are shown things that they need to accomplish in their lives. They realize the purpose of their existence and that they're being measured not by a standard of the material world but according to the real purpose of why we are here.

K. C. Armstrong: The two biggest questions in this world, in my opinion, are "What happens when we die?" and "Are we the only ones in this entire galaxy?" Do you think that possibly, when we die, we are given a choice, and we can just go to all these different places that one can only imagine?

Marilynnn Hughes: Well, there's a lot required for us to be able to go to these different places. We want and need to undergo preparation for what happens next. We don't want to waste our time while we're here. But yes, these places do exist. I can tell you this, from several experiences that I have had, when you are in heaven, there are extraterrestrials there, and it feels completely natural. Totally unremarkable until you return and it occurs to you: "Wait a minute. There were *extraterrestrials*!"

K. C. Armstrong: Yeah. They're not us!

Marilynnn Hughes: But when you're there, you don't even think about it. So yeah, aliens are there too; all the worlds converge. As we cross over, we are slowly reintegrated into this multiplicitous universe, which is so much greater than this little piece of it, this short life that we live. The thing that people don't understand is that what we regard as supernatural is not, really. It's only regarded as super-natural from where we stand in our level of evolution at this time. These mysteries are going to be recognized as totally normal and natural once our minds and spirits are more advanced.

And so, that night before I was to have my heart procedure, I was standing there with Christ, able to see my family at the same time. He's showing me how this works. You know the chart you put on the wall to see how much the children have grown?

K. C. Armstrong: Of course.

Marilynnn Hughes: Picture that. But down at the bottom is *selfishness*, and the higher up you go is more *selflessness*. Jesus was showing me that the majority of humanity is down near the bottom of the scale. He was revealing to me that this would not change if I went back. I said, "As long as it remains my choice, I have to go back to my kids."

K. C. Armstrong: He gave you a choice to pass on to this beautiful life that you just experienced, floating through all these different galaxies or going back to your family?

Marilynnn Hughes: Right. I told Him, "I'm going to pray that You will save the perfectly healthy soul that would have to die to grant me a heart transplant. I will take my chances with the heart that I've got."

All of a sudden we both were shooting through space. I knew I was going back to earth, but before I figured out what was happening, we were sitting in what looked like a bookstore. He was next to me, we were surrounded by piles of books, and they all had my name on them.

Then He was gone. When I woke up in my hospital bed I asked the doctor, "Hey, why am I still here?"

And he said, "We can't explain it, but your heart's doing a heck of a lot better today. And we don't know why."

I kept quiet because I knew why. It was literally six months later that the *Out of Body Travel Foundation* was born. After that experience with near death, I was bombarded with more out of body experiences, telling me every step that I was to take to put my plan for the Foundation into action.

It was such an amazing experience, something I'll never forget. That trip with Jesus through the many, many worlds; it's so hard to even try to describe it, but I can't wait to do that again, whenever it's time to do it permanently. It's interesting because one similarity of near death experiences is that people who go through them are not afraid of death anymore, that's for sure. Some people might be afraid of how much pain they might go through, but not of what comes afterward.

K. C. Armstrong: I see.

Marilynnn Hughes: You know, there's a certain melancholy in looking forward to the time I can return to that other realm, but first I've got work I have to do. So I guess I'd better get to it. Today, our work at the Foundation and everything that we do is an attempt to bring about as much change for the good as we possibly can on all levels of existence. We strive to relieve both physical and spiritual hunger.

K. C. Armstrong: You are surely bringing enlightenment through all your materials and sessions at the Foundation. What sorts of things are you involved in outside those doors?

Marilynnn Hughes: We try to relieve suffering all over the world. For example, in 2004 when the tsunami hit, affecting fourteen countries, we worked to reduce physical hunger worldwide because we're aware that people cannot really pursue their spiritual journey

the secret to existence is forgiveness...and the purpose of existence is to achieve selflessness

if they are dealing with physical poverty, right? Right now we're raising money for a family in Venezuela, as well as funds for about twelve young children and elderly adults that we sponsor through the *Foundation for Children In Need* in India. Over the years we've built homes, dug wells, and completed sanitation projects. We try to use the proceeds from our work to bring about as much improvement as we possibly can on all levels of existence.

Another source of positive change is my website where you can download all of our books for free. We have nine books now on the how-to process. I always recommend people begin with *Come to Wisdom's Door* and *The Mysteries of the Redemption*. Most of my readers are having experiences shortly after they read those two books, and they progress from there. There's a whole series of activities including learning to understand purification, which is necessary if you're seeking to understand an all-holy God.

K. C. Armstrong: What you have been through is very exciting and it's especially generous for you to bring your expertise to others. I'm sure you are climbing to the top of that "selflessness scale" in leaps and bounds!

Marilynnn Hughes: K. C., I have become very comfortable living in both worlds—which is really an infinite number of worlds, but that is a different expression. I have received so many graces and an inexplicable healing of my heart last year, after over fifteen years in heart failure and cardiomyopathy. An enlarged heart is not supposed to be able to go back to normal size, but mine did. A lowered Ejection Fraction should not return to normal function, but mine did. The extreme thinning of a heart wall is not supposed to return to normal thickness, but mine did—and it's not something that can happen simply through the use of medications.

K. C. Armstrong: In what way did all this change your outlook on life?

Marilynnn Hughes: I've learned that all physical reality is fluid; everything can be changed, but we don't necessarily always get to control that outcome. We have to accept God's greater will in these things. I also know that the *secret* to existence is forgiveness…and the *purpose* of existence is to achieve selflessness.

K. C. Armstrong: Marilynn, What would you tell someone else who is experiencing a major health emergency, as you did?

Marilynnn Hughes: I would say to take one step at a time, don't skip ahead. If you get a bad diagnosis, do only what you are to do next. I've seen both worlds, and whether it is life or death, your outcome will be beautiful. Death is as great an adventure as life, and life is as unpredictable as death. Everyone thinks death is the worst thing that can happen to you, but it's not. Live your life in integrity and virtue; if you do so to the best of your ability in a holy fear and love of God, death will be a welcome guest rather than a fearsome terror.

K. C. Armstrong: Marilynn, you've certainly opened our eyes to lots of new ideas to think more about. Your explanations are comforting and also exciting to consider—which is why you are one of the *World's Most Amazing Women!*

More information about Marilynn:

Website: https://outofbodytravel.org/
Book: *The Christ of the Redemption: The Mechanics of Spiritual Warfare and Energetic Alteration*
Book: *The Mysteries of the Redemption: A Treatise on Out-of Body Travel and Mysticism*

A MOTHER'S LOVE

an interview with Marcy Stone

*Marcy experienced every parent's worst nightmare,
but she has turned her tragedy into a loving benefit
for others dealing with their unspeakable grief*

INTRODUCTION:

Marcy Stone is the perfect example of something I've been the fortunate recipient of since the day I was born. I call this chapter "A Mother's Love." Marcy has two daughters that are, as far as I can ascertain, incredible people. One thing that impressed me from the start is that Marcy talks about not only providing her daughters with her unconditional love, but also learning from them. This chapter has so many lessons. Try this; do what I did. Read it first with the goal that you'll learn from Marcy and her love. Then read it again hearing Aubrey's voice. Then read it from the point of view of Sydney herself. After that, I hope you see it as I do, an unforgettable love story.

A mother can encourage her children to be champions and change the world with their compassion and love. Marcy will never be without her children, wherever she is. A mother's love is unbreakable and forever. If I am called home tomorrow, the best part of my life has been what my mother has shown me. I bet if Syd were here, she would nod—letting me know she agreed. Then she'd probably toss out a good-humored, smart-ass comment to make her sister and her mom laugh. I'm pretty sure this story will make you laugh, then cry, then go hug your mom. Here's Marcy Stone: *A Mother's Love*.

INTERVIEW:

K. C. Armstrong: I'm speaking with Marcy Stone, a certified life coach and author. Marcy has also co-founded a business, become an ordained minister, esthetician, wedding planner, and yoga teacher. Welcome, Marcy. Is there anything you don't do?

Marcy Stone: Hi, KC! I'll try anything! I am a very determined and driven person who believes that everything is possible.

K. C. Armstrong: Great! You have accomplished so much, but I know you have also experienced a heartbreak that has affected every aspect of your life. I always like to explore the qualities that make it possible to deal with life's most difficult circumstances. You have even found a way to find personal fulfillment and a sort of recovery through helping others deal with similar experiences. How and when did this inner strength take hold of you? Give us a brief overview of your childhood, if you will.

Marcy Stone: Well, as a child, I always felt as if I was being watched over or protected; that's the best way I can say it. I loved and needed my freedom, and this remains very important to me. I don't seem to have the *flight* part of the "fight or flight" mentality. I don't like the words "can't" and "no," and I'm driven to find creative solutions to any problem that might come up. Being constrained by rules would actually motivate me.

K. C. Armstrong: You'd be motivated how? To break the rules, Marcy?

Marcy Stone: Well, maybe sometimes! But I always seemed to know what I wanted and made sure I got it. I always had to do things my way. Always. I was the boss. My mom likes to tell this story about me. When I was going to preschool, she liked little frilly outfits and dressing me like a Barbie doll although, in my mind, I was anything but a Barbie doll. She took me to my first day of preschool in this fancy little dress. Now I was four years old; you could pick me up under one arm, right? When we got to school, I absolutely refused to walk through the doors. I planted myself and wasn't going anywhere. I can just picture my determined face like *absolutely not—no way, no how*! She had to pick me up, take me home, and change me into pants. Then I happily skipped back to pre-K, and that's pretty much been the story of my life. My way or the highway, unfortunately!

K. C. Armstrong: (Laughs) As you got a bit older, did you develop a passion to follow any particular field?

Marcy Stone: I don't remember ever having a profession in mind, but I wanted to be creative. I wanted to come up with new ideas and not walk in somebody else's shadow.

My parents called me a "free spirit" because I was driven by the lure of freedom; I just wanted to be on my own. Right after high school I moved out, got an apartment, and worked three jobs to make sure that I wasn't going back. I was determined to be independent, so I would say I was more motivated by that than by a career path in my youth.

K. C. Armstrong: I believe you were working in a small business when you discovered life coaching as an interest. Tell us about that.

Marcy Stone: When I was a business advisor for the firm I co-founded, we were working with a client whose employees were bringing their personal problems to the office. This obviously affected their work, and I gravitated toward those people. When I saw a life-coach training organization online, I took it because I became excited about the possibilities of helping them with the home/work connection.

K. C. Armstrong: What sorts of problems were these that affected both home and the workplace?

Marcy Stone: Very often they were life transition questions such as, "Why don't I enjoy what I'm doing for a living anymore?" or "I'm going to be an empty nester soon. How do I deal with that?" It seems clients often find me after I've had an experience similar to the very thing they want to discuss. I believe the universe brings you what you can handle, and so it helps to have the experience to understand where they're coming from (not necessarily to impose my solution on them).

K. C. Armstrong: I want to talk next about the topic of motherhood because it's a pivotal part of your story and your book, as well. You've had a really amazing journey into motherhood. I have people I love and care about, but I've heard that a mother's love is something irreplaceable, and its bond is beyond special.

Marcy Stone: Your observation is a hundred percent true and actually brings me to tears.

K. C. Armstrong: Growing up, many girls are given baby dolls and can't wait to be a mom. Was that what you experienced as a child?

Marcy Stone: Going way back, I have to say, no. I wasn't playing with those dolls; I played with trucks. Actually, we blew up Barbie dolls in the sandbox! I found crawfish and brought them home. (My mom always made me take them back). It never dawned on me that I might someday be a mom.

K. C. Armstrong: I know that almost wasn't a possibility for you; you went through some pretty serious things at sixteen including laser surgeries for cervical cancer. What was it like to hear the word *cancer* at such a young age, and how did that affect your views on motherhood?

Marcy Stone: I was only sixteen, so the cancer diagnosis didn't ring serious; it really didn't. They called it *dysplasia early stage*. Not a big deal. So I just went to the doctor repeatedly for these little laser surgeries. I was twenty or twenty-one though when the doctors told me I couldn't have children. I'll have to admit neither my boyfriend nor I were too upset about that news. We both were just having a good time with no thoughts about our future, let alone having children.

K. C. Armstrong: And then you got that surprise that—Wow!—you are pregnant! What was that like when you both had planned on living your lives in a whole different way?

Marcy Stone: My first response was, "That can't be right! Go back and check the test again. You made a mistake. This is not possible!" When I look back at it, I'm disappointed in myself. In my defense, I was very immature. I believe that a child can feel your emotions from conception, so I really tried to make up for that first reaction throughout the rest of the pregnancy.

About half way through, the doctors told us I was carrying twins but that one of the babies wasn't doing well. At about seven and a half months they said *he* wasn't going to make it. It happened in such a quick span of weeks; we hadn't even wrapped our heads around the fact that we were having twins before we had to deal with the news that we would lose one. It was just so surreal, it really was. Using the pronoun *he* made both children seem more real to us.

Next they informed us that the girl, Aubrey, wasn't going to make it, either. They told us she had "issues"—a hole in her heart and spinal bifida. We even did an amnio, where they stick a needle down through your belly. That was awful. I don't recommend it! They took Level Four ultrasounds, but they couldn't show me the spine or the hole in her heart. They advised me to abort the pregnancy, but I told them, "Absolutely not; that is NOT happening. There's nothing wrong with this child. You guys are crazy!" And sure enough, Aubrey was born perfectly healthy—a beautiful, healthy baby girl.

I call her my *angel baby.* She never got sick, and everything about her was picture perfect—and still is. Maybe I'm biased, but she was an amazing and fabulous way to be introduced to parenting; I had never even held a baby before. Somebody in the hospital said, "Hold her like a football." I don't play or watch football—never have! Aubrey really made learning how to parent super easy, though. She really did.

K. C. Armstrong: Now something happened when Aubrey was three, and I've heard women say that sometimes it takes an event like this to make them really feel the weight and seriousness of motherhood. Can you tell us a little bit about what happened to Aubrey?

Marcy Stone: Sure. She's going to love this! It was the defining moment for me between being a mom and becoming what I call "a mama bear." That phrase, to me, means so much. When Aubrey was just shy of three, she fell halfway down a flight of stairs. I'm not a bad mom, I swear. She just tripped, fell and hit her head against the side of the wall. She started to cry immediately, and I kicked right into gear. I scooped her up with a towel to catch the blood, in front of a houseful of people, and said, "OK, Aubrey, we're going for a ride!"

Thankfully, we lived only five minutes from the emergency room. After a quick look at her injury, the doctor took her to the back and prepped her for stitches. I told her to keep looking at me. *Watch my eyes. See how calm I am.* I didn't use those words, but she picked up on the lack of panic, and the doctor was floored. It was at that moment that I realized, "Wow. I have this incredible influence over this little being. She has that much trust in me even when she's in pain. She knows she's feeling something, but *Mom says it's OK, so I'm good. I'm golden.*

That is an incredible power and responsibility to have with another human being. And it was at that moment that I realized what my role was with this little person. It was life changing for me. She needed me, and at the same time she schooled me on how to be a "mama bear." It was really remarkable.

K. C. Armstrong: Marcy, you listed three things in your book on becoming a *mama bear*, and they stuck with me. You wrote, "Be brave but feel; be strong but know your limits; and trust your instincts." Great advice for a mother or for anyone caring for another person of any age.

Marcy Stone: I think it's super important that you live those words because your children emulate your every move. They're watching, hiding on top of the steps listening to the conversation. They're not missing anything. Being aware and setting the best example always is the difference between just going through the motions and being a mamma bear, in my opinion.

K. C. Armstrong: Tell us now, if you will, about your second daughter, Sydney.

Marcy Stone: My pregnancy with my second daughter, Sydney, was so much easier! From very young, Sydney was pretty, incredibly outgoing, and witty with a very dry sense of humor. She was the yin to my yang, if you will. I had a relationship with both of my daughters that a lot of people would envy. The girls made sure that we kept our close relationship, and I made sure that we were all really trying. Sydney was the glue for us in a lot of different situations. She was my mini-me, but she left this world much too soon, at only twenty-one years old.

K. C. Armstrong: I'm so sorry, Marcy. Please share with us some of your memories of Sydney.

Marcy Stone: Every memory is phenomenal, even the moments when we didn't all see eye-to-eye. I mean there were three females in the house, so arguments were bound to happen, right? But it was usually Sydney that broke it up. She would sing, "*WHY CAN'T WE BE FRIENDS...*" at the top of her lungs or some other silly thing to get us all laughing.

Aubrey and I were completely happy to let Syd shine her light brightly. She was so much fun, and she usually wanted to be the jokester. She had such a powerful presence and was such a joy to be around; who wouldn't want her taking the lead role? It was so easy for her. She kept everyone in her path smiling.

K. C. Armstrong: As a mother, you couldn't ask for more, right?

Marcy Stone: Right. She had it all. Sydney was crazy cool. You would have loved her. Everybody that knew her loved her. She used to tease me that she was going to be with me until she was ninety-five. I was totally cool with that! Absolutely. I mean that would have been the best gift anybody could ever have because we did just about every-thing together. Her friends were my friends, and that was really fab-ulous. She was starting to branch out and make some new ones, but she would always make sure I felt included. Syd packed so much into twenty-one years of life. She really did, including traveling a good bit of the world. She had a serious boyfriend for a while, and I'm really grateful that she had the opportunity to feel that love.

K. C. Armstrong: Did you like the boyfriend? I'm sure someone good enough for your daughter is impossible to find. A mother's love, Right?

Marcy Stone: Absolutely! A mother's love! (laughs) But she was very wise early on. She called one afternoon to tell me about her relationship, "Mom, I don't think this is working. I think I need to come back home." Well, I'm on the other side of the phone jumping up and down trying to hide my excitement saying, "Well, if you think that's the right decision honey…" We spent every bit of time together that we could, up until her very last day.

K. C. Armstrong: Marcy, can you tell us about the terrible day that you lost her?

Marcy Stone: I will try to do that without getting choked up. My daughter Sydney was twenty-one years and three months old. She went out with friends on Christmas Eve and was the passenger in a motor vehicle that was involved in an accident caused by a drunk driver.

Before returning from work that day she had forewarned me, "Mom, I think I might want to go out and celebrate my friend's birthday." Now Sydney wasn't a drinker; that wasn't important to either of my girls, but she liked to be with people and was very social. I told her, "Absolutely, go!"

She texted before leaving work for the day, "Hey, Mom. I don't know; maybe I'm not going to go." I knew she was looking for my permission. It was always about, "Is Mom good with what I do? Are we copacetic?" She would never, ever do anything that she thought I wasn't going to approve of.

She had been excited about the birthday celebration all week. I told her, "Honey, this is something that you want to do. You have my blessing. Absolutely. Go have a good time, and just please be safe."

So she went out with a friend who introduced her to some of his other friends. They all had a good time together. Sydney had a zero alcohol blood level that afternoon, but the driver had alcohol in his system. They were out on a four wheeler, and the four wheeler was hit by a car. Sydney's skull was fractured, and she didn't make it. The driver was in a coma for a little while. He eventually made a full recovery. But Sydney is not with us anymore.

Twenty-one years and three months. As a mother, you have to try and find ways to cope. I know she was having fun. Still, you're drawn to that last moment. *What was she thinking? What was she feeling? Did she see it coming? Did she suffer?*

> **I heard her soft voice: "I'm safe. I'm sorry. I love you.**

I still have to wake myself up in the middle of the night sometimes because I go back to the most painful day of my life-when I had to go to the hospital morgue to identify her body.

I looked at Sydney lying there, so peaceful, so beautiful. I kissed her forehead and I held her. Then, all of a sudden, I heard her soft voice: "I'm safe. I'm sorry. I love you." And that's been like a mantra for me ever since that moment.

From that moment at the morgue throughout the following days, I was torn. "Do I want to do this? Do I not want to do this?" But I know if I hadn't had that closure, that visual of her, that last kiss on her forehead, I would have regretted it for the rest of my life. So as painful and as hard as it was, there's no regret.

K. C. Armstrong: Wait a minute. Go back. You actually heard Sydney's voice?

Marcy Stone: I heard it loud and clear: *I'm safe. I'm sorry. I love you.*

K. C. Armstrong: "I'm sorry"?

Marcy Stone: I'm sorry. I'm sorry that it happened. I'm sorry that I was out. I'm sorry that I'm gone.

K. C. Armstrong: Even this says so much about Sydney's character.

Marcy Stone: Absolutely. She worried about me. But I am super grateful for every single moment with Syd. And I'll tell you what; it's those moments… all of those memories, that get me through every day. Today was a hard day for me. I woke up this morning angry, and I work very hard to allow the anger because if I don't, I'm going to burst at the seams. But I have to allow it in healthy ways. I can't let anger take me down an ugly path. So I wrote a little bit about it. I was angry because my oldest daughter is going to be twenty-six tomorrow, and I know she's thinking the same thing I am: "Here we go. Another family celebration where we're missing someone. It is not the same." I woke up that way today because I can't be that way tomorrow, if that makes sense. I need to be all I can for my daughter, Aubrey. She needs to see that.

K. C. Armstrong: Of course it makes perfect sense. This is a mother's worst nightmare. Did you go to any groups or find some kind of support? I don't see how you could take this on yourself. Tell me about how you got to be able to feel somewhat normal.

Marcy Stone: Still working on the *somewhat normal* part. There were no groups or books that resonated with me even then. From the beginning, though, I really truly did listen to Sydney's guidance. She was insistent that I keep a journal. She told me to stay in the pain, as crazy as that sounds. When you don't, you close your heart which just prolongs the healing process. It's the love that you have for the person you lost that helps get you through the hardest moments.

K. C. Armstrong: How was Sydney able to guide you through your grief?

Marcy Stone: Shortly after she was taken from us, she started coming to me in my dreams. "Mom, you've got to journal." She still says it to me. I took a little break for a while and she told me, "Mom, you gotta feel the pain. You have to lean into it. Love is what is gonna get you through this." Journaling is definitely helping.

K. C. Armstrong: And all of this pain is what led you to share your insights with others in your book, *The Voice of an Angel: a Mother's Guide to Grief and How to Thrive After the Loss of a Child.*

Marcy Stone: Yes. It gives me great comfort to pass along what I have experienced and learned since Sydney left us. I think a lot of people don't know where to turn. It's satisfying that I can help someone who might find my book in their moment of tragedy.

K. C. Armstrong: It's so fortunate that you've been able to connect with your daughter on another level. The way you describe being able to hear what your daughter's telling you about how to get through this is amazing and encouraging.

Marcy Stone: Before this, I never really put much thought into what we call death. Most people are afraid. They don't want to talk about it; they don't want to think about it. It's not necessarily something that I would have picked to consider deeply or write about. But this is the card I was dealt. I have to make the most of my life. Sydney would be throwing stuff at me if she thought that I was settling, not living my purpose, or not giving back the way I always did. I absolutely never wanted to let her down when she was here, and I certainly don't want to let her down now that she is in heaven watching me.

In the very beginning of my book are the details of what took place, how I experienced it, and basically what I remember. I wrote it down immediately, and then the journaling and steps that I took after that. I share my thoughts at the time: What was the most important thing for me to do? How do you get through a funeral or something like that? How do you think logically at a time when there is no logic?

The journaling actually brought me to realizing there is an intrinsic, natural logic. We don't recognize it because in death we push it down. It's easier to be numb than it is to feel the loss. Sydney was guiding me to do the exact opposite of what I wanted to do. And she's right. She was right here on earth, and she is right on the other side. Facing the pain actually has been the saving grace for me. I don't know that I would be sitting here talking to you right now otherwise.

K. C. Armstrong: What other insights can you offer someone that is going through something like this?

Marcy Stone: Hopefully someone will have your best interests at heart to help you make decisions for a while. You can go back to them months later and discover what really happened. In the beginning you have little recollection of details because you must focus on establishing *why* you are going to move forward. Why will I continue my life?

I'm sad to say that you go there, but when you lose a child you do. What is my purpose at this point? Why am I going to take my next breath? Some people actually have survivor's guilt, you know. But it was then that I established my *raison d'être*—my reason for being. I have another daughter. She absolutely needs me now more than ever. I can't fail her.

I put my energy into that and the love that Sydney was telling me would help me heal from this. It's not like you don't lament. It's just that—I'm still a mom. I'm still a mama bear. I still have this responsibility. I'm actually really grateful to have had that guidance because it saw me through to being able to journal, write the book, and stay present in all of it.

K. C. Armstrong: What was the time frame like for you to begin moving forward?

Marcy Stone: The writing part, the journaling, was helpful from the beginning. Looking through my notes, it was April or May, four or five months after her death, that Sydney came to me in a dream tapping her foot, holding a pen and paper and saying, "Mom, come on. Let's go! We got stuff to do! Mama, go back to your journaling!"

I'm thinking, "You gotta be kidding me! I am not ready for this yet!" But I realized, wow, look at that—she's right. That's when I really got serious about going forward.

K. C. Armstrong: What were some of the first things that you wrote about?

Marcy Stone: Basic fundamentals, like what I need to do to survive. What I need to do to take care of me in order to be able to get to the next level. What to do when I wake up tomorrow; that's where it started. What I missed about Syd, and how the girls were raised.

The chapters started to develop fairly easily. I would just write about love and then I would write about compassion, not only for myself, but also for the individuals in the accident. For the court system, too. Trust me, you need to have a lot of compassion for the court system. Finally, the thoughts started to almost light up on the page. I had so much guidance.

K. C. Armstrong: Did you know from the start that your writing would become a book?

Marcy Stone: Sydney told me loud and clear! I knew. But let me just make a point here. She's always been a little bossy, and it was one of the things Aubrey and I found so endearing about her. Syd may be the youngest, but she kind of ruled the roost—such a beautiful, bright, bossy light! She told me I was to write this book because there are people out there that are experiencing the same thing I'm going through. They are like-minded and aren't going to have a place to turn. So, she said, I have to make sure that they have what they need. So yeah, she was very clear.

K. C. Armstrong: It seems that Sydney's strong personality, but also your ability to listen, is what made this beneficial wisdom from the other side possible.

Marcy Stone: I am truly blessed, and I often wonder what people that don't have the same kind of faith or belief do in a situation like this. I cannot even imagine not having that voice with its comfort and guidance. That's got to be really hard.

K. C. Armstrong: Did writing this book, or the entire experience, teach you anything you did not previously know about yourself?

Marcy Stone: I did not know I would have the strength to survive losing a child because my children have always been, and will continue to be, my reason for being.

There are hard days and easy days. There are all kinds of days in between. Every once in a while I question whether I won't hear from her anymore now that the book is done. And then she does something crazy and I hear her: "Mama, I'm not going anywhere. You got stuff to do. We're not done yet."

On the hard days I sometimes visit my go-to emotion, anger. Then I have to allow myself to feel the true emotion of whatever grief is trying to consume me. I remind myself that when I'm angry I can't hear Syd. She goes away, almost like she's punishing me. That's my motivation to move through the anger faster. I found a way to trick myself!

K. C. Armstrong: I like that phrase, actually. I think a lot of times we have to trick ourselves into pulling out of these negative emotions because otherwise we'll just convince ourselves that this is where we need to be. We need to stay sad, or we need to stay angry when really we're stronger than that. You are an example of the strength we can find in ourselves when we absolutely need it.

Marcy Stone: I've never been one for compliments, but when someone tells me I'm strong, I take it, absorb it, and hang on to it. I have this inner bulletin board, if you will. There are days I need to tack up that complement of strength as a reminder to myself. Somebody says, "Oh, you're really strong." What they don't know is that today I needed that. Thank you. I hang on to it. It's like my reserve tank.

K. C. Armstrong: What do you consider qualities that have been most beneficial to approaching peace and acceptance? Qualities someone in a similar situation should try to grasp?

Marcy Stone: That's a really good question. Big one. The first trait I think of is kindness, to yourself. I always say, "no regrets, no grudges, no guilt." Those three no's are all pointless. As human beings and as a society we tend to rake ourselves over the coals. How could I have done it better? How could I have done it differently? It's pointless. Why would you take yourself through that if you did the best you could do?

Forgiveness is also greatly important. In losing a child to an auto accident, it's natural to want to know, "OK, who's responsible? Who took my child's life?" Pass the blame; hold the grudge and never forgive that individual. All of those things are doing nothing to anybody other than yourself. It's like you have this backpack and you're loading these huge boulders and carrying them around with you. It's hurting your back and the ache only grows. It's terrible for the mind, terrible for the heart.

I'd say forgiveness is probably the biggest contribution in making peace within yourself after a tragedy. And then you can always count on karma. Yes, I'm a big believer in karma; it's choice and consequence, right?

If you make a choice to do X Y and Z, there is a consequence associated with that. The karma you create will absolutely come back to you. I don't need to know what or when it is. So for me, forgiveness is allowing myself to let go. I'm not going to forget my anger, but I'm also not going to carry it. I mention that throughout multiple chapters of my book because it's so important to your own sanity. I could not sleep well at night, nor could I hear my daughter's voice if I were not forgiving. I couldn't take notice of the ladybug or the butterfly or the obscure music groups Sydney loved that now seem to inexplicably surround me.

So we all have our own personal way of making peace after tragedy, and those have been really important to me. It might be different for somebody else. But the girls and I talked all the time about living a life with no regrets, and I can honestly say to you now, having lost Sydney, that I can look back and say I have no regrets.

K. C. Armstrong: I don't know many people that can say that. You are helping so many people today and through your book, Marcy. I know the good karma you produce each day will bring you much compassion and happiness in the future.

Marcy Stone: Thank you so much for letting me share my memories of Sydney with you. I truly hope my book can ease the burden of others who are where I was. Syd told me, "Don't stop living, Mama. Live through this. You will feel good again, I promise!" She promised, so I stayed open. I hope others will, too.

K. C. Armstrong: We've learned so much from you today, Marcy. You've given us a glimpse of unimaginable grief, but also the encouragement that we are resilient enough to work through it. You've given both your daughters such a rare and positive outlook on life and on finding their own "raison d'être." For all these reasons, we celebrate you as one of the *World's Most Amazing Women!*

More information about Marcy:

Website: www.marcystone.com
Book: *The Voice of an Angel*
Books: *The Best of Both Worlds Cookbook,* Volumes 1, 2 & 3 by Ken Bell and Marcy Stone

8

LIVE YOUR PASSIONS

an interview with Sandi Holst

Sandi Holst reminds us that we should spend every
day doing what we love—even at work

INTRODUCTION:

Sandi Holst's story is an example of how one's life can change drastically in an instant. During the final edits of this book, her husband of forty years passed away unexpectedly. Having gotten to know Sandi, my staff and I were crushed. I remember asking Sandi one day about her husband, Herb, and she revealed to me that he had a favorite place that he loved. I asked if she would show it to me, and she sent me a beautiful picture that I immediately made the computer background in my office.

When it was time to sign off on the final cover design for this book, that picture seemed to epitomize the whole tone and message we are trying to create. I felt that placing that photo of Herb's favorite place on the cover would somehow honor both Sandi and Herb. I knew it spoke our truth about the depth of human goodness, and it made me certain that Herb would be looking over this project and sharing the experience with Sandi. Most of all, I wanted my friend to smile.

INTERVIEW:

K. C. Armstrong: Our next guest is a self-described "passion junkie" who can amaze us all with her stories of rock climbing, hiking, biking, scuba diving, and even skydiving! But Sandi Holst is also an author, an entrepreneur and a business coach. This woman's energy and passion are unparalleled, so it's with great honor I introduce you to Sandi Holst. Welcome, Sandi! How are you today?

Sandi Holst: Doing really great, K. C. I've recently moved from a big city to a small tourist town that we've been visiting for thirty years. Since then I've started a new type of business mentoring other people to live their passions. I wrote a book called *Breathe! You Got This*. PLUS, I honed my photography skills and guess what? This year I got into an art gallery.

K. C. Armstrong: Sounds like you're on fire! Where does all this energy and momentum come from?

Sandi Holst: My mandate is to simply live your passions. If that somehow includes your business life, that's even better because we want to spend every moment of the day being happy and doing what we love. I believe in life being an adventure and in throwing yourself into activities that inspire you. If the day-to-day routine of your job is not satisfying, then you may have to get out there and grab some excitement in your life.

K. C. Armstrong: I agree that it's important to make your work life a part of your overall quest for happiness. So many people look at the life they want to live as a *result* of their work life or as *separate* from their work life. What do you do if you aren't enjoying yourself at work?

Sandi Holst: Many of us were guided to the safest careers possible. When I started high school, my guidance counselor asked what career path I thought I'd like to follow. I gave him some crazy ideas, and he actually told me, "No, no, no, Darling. I think you would do really well as a bookkeeper, a nurse, or a housewife." Really! I did consider nursing for a time because I think it's a fabulous career choice, but I have an issue with bodily fluids so I wasn't going to go in that direction! I've been in the hospital once or twice, and all the power to those wonderful people that look after you.

However, many people are finding that those "safe" jobs do not necessarily lead to happiness in the workplace. By feeling we have to be "safe," too often we end up being unhappy, and next thing you know we're forty and having a midlife crisis. It's important to learn that we don't have to be safe; we can grow and evolve throughout our working lives.

K. C. Armstrong: That's commendable, Sandi. We all spend a lot of time at work. What happens to people after they've been in a job for a few years? We call it "burn-out," but what does that really mean?

Sandi Holst: My take on it is this: typically, in your twenties and thirties, you take the "sensible" job, work at it for a few years, and find yourself thinking, "I dread going to work." It could be burnout, as you say, which is mostly boredom, or maybe you were not suited to that particular job right from the beginning. That's especially true when people choose a job or career path on the basis of salary or schedule only.

As they say, *We have only one life to live, and it's not a dress rehearsal.* Once you get into your fifties, you think of that cliché more and more. But we have to learn to react to dissatisfaction faster. I'll tell you, I'm one of the people in the trenches that did not like a lot of things about my job. I was going from job to job thinking, "Oh my. This is crazy!" Looking back, why couldn't I have reacted faster?

I had one job for about twelve years. I remember coming home and thinking, "Is this all there is to life?" I worked eight hour shifts. You would never see me in my office one minute before or after I was supposed to be there. I was only working for a paycheck. Afterwards, I would get on my bike or go hiking or rock climbing. It was heart wrenching sometimes, realizing I had been talking for so long about making some sort of change but not doing anything about it.

K. C. Armstrong: Once you realized you were miserable at work, what helped you to make the leap between what you knew was safe or familiar to something new and perhaps risky?

Sandi Holst: By 2001, I had suffered working for three horrible bosses in a row. I was starting to think, "I can do better than this! If I had staff, I would most certainly treat them better than I'm being treated." I was fed up and I guess that's what finally made me act. I chose something that I knew, which was bookkeeping and account- ing. I started off with basic bookkeeping, looking after people and closing out their books.

Next thing I knew, I was getting a free education from accountants because they appreciated my skill level. The more I knew, the better for them. Before long, I was a high-level bookkeeper with clients in Japan, China, Germany, U.S.A and quite financially abundant with my business.

K. C. Armstrong: That's definitely an accomplishment. There was a personal factor, too. The close relationship you built with your associates while helping each other led to your becoming a business coach, right?

Sandi Holst: Yes. It's really weird. This is when I realized that this was the path I was supposed to follow. My colleagues were corporate lawyers and accountants; my clients were all amazing people in different industries with great ideas. They had worldwide sales in the millions each year and it seemed they were hardly working for it. Meanwhile, I'm learning so much from all of my clients and colleagues. I'm picking up what to do and what not to do to be successful. I learned how to pass on this information to shorten the learning curve for others. Being in business is tough. It's not for the faint-hearted, but it doesn't have to be that way. If you can help people become successful in one or two years instead of five, they can get out of the trenches that much faster.

K. C. Armstrong: True. How did you feel when you were finally out of the environment of unpleasant bosses and doing something that created financial success for yourself and the people you worked with?

Sandi Holst: It was fabulous! I was passionate about the growth I was seeing. We all desire to make money on our passions, but we have this fear of not being able to support ourselves. What if it doesn't work? While you're thinking of making changes, months and possibly years could pass. But if all of a sudden you find a reason that you just *have* to do it, you recognize your true direction. That is what happened to me.

After all those bad experiences I knew I had to change. All of a sudden things became easier. I knew I was heading in my true direction because clients came out of the blue without me even pushing that hard. In the thirteen years that followed, I learned a lot and I led staff and clients to success. At the end of that time period I saw another light bulb switch on, and this time I wasn't fearful to move from one business to another.

K. C. Armstrong: You developed the confidence to break out of the routine that previously kept you "safe."

Sandi Holst: Exactly. One thing I advise is to separate yourself from the naysayers. It's great if you want to get somebody else's opinion about making changes in your life, but choose who you share your dreams with carefully. Make sure that person is open-minded and not caught in the web of sameness themselves.

K. C. Armstrong: Sandi, did your childhood or background some-how prepare you for this philosophy that work should be an integral part of a happy life rather than a chore to be endured?

Sandi Holst: I'd say probably, yes. Ours was a low income family. However, I never knew it until I became an adult. We had a roof over our heads, food on the table, and clothes on our backs. We lived in a safe neighborhood and I had lots of friends to play with. My parents, grandparents and relatives were all doing the best they could under the circumstances of their own upbringings, but I can't count how many times we were told:

"Money doesn't grow on trees."

"I know you want to be a doctor, but that costs money we don't have. How about you train to be a secretary, receptionist, bookkeeper or— better yet—*marry* the doctor instead?"

I think *wanting* and never *getting* goes back many generations in many families, including mine. I am hoping I broke that mold. In my adult life I've worked very hard to get what I want. Very hard! But you have to keep your inner happiness while doing that.

K. C. Armstrong: I'm sure you have plenty of advice for any of my listeners or readers who may be feeling stuck. What's your advice to them on finding their passion?

Sandi Holst: I always say the first step is to find out what's stifling your ambitions. You have these passions in your head, you think about them all the time, and you wish you could be making money from them. You have to find out why you are afraid to move forward. It is in your best interest to take baby steps. However, ensure that you do move forward; simply do it at your own pace. You do not need to quit your current job right away. Spend time each week researching and taking small steps. You will know when you are ready to make the jump. Even searching the internet to find others in business who mesh with your interests is a step forward.

Step two is to plan what you are going to do to reach those ambitions. It's really important not to try to control the end result. For example, maybe you are dreaming of a particular high-end house in the perfect neighborhood. You know of at least five ways you could go about getting it. However, the Universe has another 300 million ways that you haven't thought of. Therefore, you don't want to control the way your dream will come to fruition. It is your job to envision what you desire, take steps in getting it, and then let it go. We simply can't fathom all the different possibilities that could make it come to reality.

K. C. Armstrong: As a business coach who wants to see people be successful while making full use of their strongest interests, how do you begin helping a new client?

Sandi Holst: I ask the client to take five minutes each morning before getting out of bed, or perhaps sitting in a comfy chair, and envision their ideal life. Do you see an improved personal life, business life, or both? If you envision a truck, what color is it? What kind is it? Is it a GMC or Ford? Be generous with your detailing.

Really go into detail in that five minutes. No more than five, because then you'll start daydreaming and stray off topic. Again, be specific. If you want to have a million dollars in a bank account, a house near a river, or perhaps the best condo in your favorite city, then envision the details. Once the five minutes is over, open your eyes and move on with your day.

Then say to yourself, "What one or two things am I going to do today to work to that end result?" Do this for five minutes every single day. The more you focus on this goal and today's step or steps in that direction, the more it's going to become reality.

K. C. Armstrong: It's like a gravitational pull, right? Whatever you focus on becomes your reality. If you're focusing on the negative, you're going to have a negative life. But if you're focusing on the positive and the good things that are actually happening in your life, you'll change your mentality

Sandi Holst: Sure. Self-help gurus talk about the Law of Attraction. Let's say, for example, you have a forty thousand dollar line of credit that never seems to come down, and you keep using it. Don't focus on forty thousand; instead, focus on zero. It may sound weird, but envision zero. This is what you want to see. So that's the Law of Attraction, but we have a tendency to expect the worst end result. We see that balance, and we hate it, we hate it! But guess what we're focusing on? Again, we're focusing on the balance when we should be focusing on that statement showing zero due. Keeping our attention there will attract the will to make that zero balance become reality.

K. C. Armstrong: To be clear, picturing the zero isn't going to make it appear, right? I think your point is to focus on what we want, rather than what we don't want, to happen. Just a different way of looking at things.

Sandi Holst: That's exactly right.

K. C. Armstrong: I understand that your experiences as an accountant and working with so many successful entrepreneurs showed you the way to get ahead, but you must have had other influences or mentors. Is that so?

Sandi Holst: That is most certainly the case. Actually, my life changed the day that Dr. Wayne Dyer passed away.

K. C. Armstrong: I'm not familiar with him.

> *Sometimes you just have to wake up and feel that slap in the face from the universe saying you need to go in another direction.*

Sandi Holst: Wayne Dyer was a very popular self-help author and motivational speaker and was called "the Father of Motivation." He wrote many inspiring books and was a regular on TV, radio shows and YouTube. Through a quirk of fate I found out he is a distant relative of mine, and on the day his passing was in the news, I started asking questions about him and reading his books. This opened up the self-help genre to me, and suddenly I was on a whole new path. This is what prompted me to move from a big city to a tiny little town with only eight hundred people and create a mentorship business.

Though it was important at the time, if I still owned my accounting business I would have been buried at my computer keyboard. Day in and day out, sixteen hours a day. Sometimes you just have to wake up and feel that slap in the face from the universe saying you need to go in another direction. Wayne Dyer was a wake-up call for me.

K. C. Armstrong: The world is changing and we have to allow ourselves to change, too.

Sandi Holst: Right. For example, last week I worked with a woman from California who now lives in a cold state with no shoreline. She wanted to continue to work at the job she knew, but her passion was to live on the beach. Well, with today's technology almost anything is possible! We worked to make her industry computer-based so she can be working with her clients from anywhere. Now, if she chooses to relocate to the place of her dreams, she can work right from the beach with her computer!

K. C. Armstrong: So you don't have to save what you love the most for the weekends. You can actually enjoy it all the time!

Sandi Holst: It's so interesting. I live on this little peninsula where there's a prevalent mindset that everyone should be an employee in one of the small local businesses. I try to push people here to see outside of the box. We're immersed in technology now. Your clients aren't within a fifty kilometer circle; they may even be in another country! You know your product or service can go anywhere. Your clients can be worldwide now, and we have to think about that. I'm still in the accounting industry with some clients that I've had for almost twenty years. With technology and computers, I can jump into a program and mentor them or offer business services in the comfort of my home in my PJ's and bunny slippers.

K. C. Armstrong: Nice! That makes me wonder why we all don't put more emphasis on happiness when we are searching for a career. It doesn't seem to get factored in! I like the whole on-the-beach and bunny slippers idea.

Sandi Holst: (laughs) I tell you, K.C., learning to follow my passion without worry has sent me in a completely different direction than I ever expected. I've learned to be open to opportunities I never would have considered before. It's really freeing.

K. C. Armstrong: I couldn't agree with you more. To be able to combine your passions and responsibilities—how awesome! Let's say you have a love for photography; there has to be a way to incorporate that love with making money.

Sandi Holst: That's the point, exactly. If you have a passion for looking after kids, looking after dogs, creating art—anything, any weird idea that you have, there are people in the world that will buy it.

K. C. Armstrong: Would you consider your book a road map to figure out how to make your passion a reality and make money at the same time?

Sandi Holst: It is. Don't worry about competition when you're passionate about what you do because you'll provide more than what your client or customer is looking for. There is no competition because you're all in—and it shows.

The biggest problem I see is the fear of failure. People will say, "What if I fail?" So right at the start, you're thinking about failure. What we have to do is learn to change this mindset; look at how wonderful your life will be when you take control, and you're getting paid your true value. That's the key: to change that mindset. Of course it's difficult when you have to make a living, but remember the Law of Attraction.

K. C. Armstrong: How do people generally respond to your advice?

Sandi Holst: I've had people come up and give me hugs and say, "Thank you, thank you, thank you!" I'm proud to say that even professionals in the field have responded with enthusiasm. So, yes, I'm loving this journey! I talked about writing a book for a long time, and I have to practice what I preach. If there's something that's been on my list, then I've got to just get it done.

K. C. Armstrong: Sandi, you've taken us through a familiar story: a boring day at work, making dinner, some TV, and bedtime before the alarm rings to start over again. But you've shown us that with guidance, thought and some motivation, we can make the most of our lives, enjoying our days so much more. This advice is a great gift. If you could speak directly to our listeners and readers, what would you most like to tell them?

Sandi Holst: I'd explain that I have lived that unfulfilled life, and it wasn't until I was fifty years old that I started questioning why. Now I am open to a great many things, including spirituality. I would love to say to your listeners and readers: once you truly believe in yourself, you are halfway to your destination. A positive mind equals a positive life. That's what I want you to remember. Also, I dare you to dream, but more importantly, I dare you to *act* on your dreams.

You can get past all your challenges. Life is a journey and we are all here to experience the best times that come our way. Instead of choosing to struggle, pick another direction. It is easier and more rewarding. Keep on learning how to change your mindset and get the life you desire. That's the journey! Learn and, most importantly, apply.

K. C. Armstrong: Very helpful, Sandi. How much happier the world would be if we all followed your example! It's not selfish to want to enjoy each day of our lives to the extent we can. Thank you so much for sharing your wisdom and for being, without a doubt, one of the *World's Most Amazing Women*.

More information about Sandi:

Website: SandiHolst.com
Book: *Breathe, You Got This*

A SONG OF GRATITUDE

an interview with Dr. Feyi Obamehinti

Meeting her abusive mother for the first time at age sixteen helped Dr. Obamehinit develop a deep appreciation for family closeness

INTRODUCTION:

After suffering traumatic abuse at the hands of a family member, Dr. Feyi Obamehinti surrendered her life to Jesus Christ. She has written Christian books describing her journey to Christ and the hope that she has because of Him. She wants to spread this message to all who have suffered abuse. Her grandfather was a minister; her grandmother was a school principal, and through them she learned responsibility and structure as well as having a safe space from others' abuse.

She found even more strength in her Christian beliefs by founding an organization to help people from different countries assimilate into American society while holding on to their culture's values. My whole staff loves when she calls the station because the kindness and genuine concern she shows confirms that positive people are out there, and when you meet one, it brightens your day.

INTERVIEW:

K. C. Armstrong: Our next guest is a wife, mother, ordained minister, speaker, and author. She is also the co-founder of the non-profit organization *Oasis Focus Incorporated* and regularly hosts *Oasis Connection*, a Christian TV show. Dr. Obamehinti, how are you today?

Dr. Feyi Obamehinti: I am doing very well. I am so excited to be a part of your team here at WMAP Radio.

K. C. Armstrong: And we are delighted and privileged to speak with you today. We'll be talking about the need so many people have of knowing how to deal with struggles every day. Too many of us get caught up in obsessive or abusive habits, not knowing where to turn. I know you have an amazing story of abuse, discovery, and healing. But before we get to all you've learned, let's get to know a bit about your background. I believe you were born in Phoenix but somehow wound up in Nigeria. How did that come about?

Dr. Feyi Obamehinti: Well yes, I was born in Phoenix, AZ of Nigerian parents who were in the U.S. to go to University in the late 60s. After I was born, things didn't work out between them, so I was sent to their native Nigeria at six months old by myself on a sixteen hour flight. Both my parents remarried so there was a bit of a shuffle about who should raise me, the only child between them. My paternal grandparents claimed me, and so I grew up with them in Nigeria where they both showered me with love and provided me with a stable home and a good education. But at that point I did not know that my grandparents were really not my actual parents. I grew up believing I was their number seven child, since they had six children before I arrived, and I had no way of knowing that wasn't so.

My paternal grandfather was an African Methodist minister and alternative medicine doctor, and my grandmother was a retired school principal. God used both of these amazing people to set great examples for me, and I went to elementary, middle, high school and three years of university in Nigeria before moving back to the U.S.

During the transition from high school into college, something remarkable happened. I was invited to a youth camp by my biology teacher, with whom I had a very good relationship. It was at this camp that my life radically changed. Because my grandfather was a minister, I went to church as a child, but that was about it. There was really no strong relationship with an eternal God with the impact of what that could mean in my life.

But God is so great that He makes sure that every single thing that happens in our life is part of the overall action plan that He has for us. At camp I experienced what is called a "defining moment," which is something that changes us and marks us for life. I'm so grateful that I gave my heart and life to Jesus Christ then, because that was my foundation for everything that has happened since.

K. C. Armstrong: It's interesting that when we have these "defining moments," we don't always recognize their importance while we are going through them. Was that the case?

Dr. Feyi Obamehinti Oh yes, that is very, very true! You look back and say Wow! This is where my life found its true meaning! I understood for the first time that religion is not just about going to church. It is about establishing a relationship with God through His Son, Jesus Christ. Jesus Christ loves me so much that He died for me. Now if I accept Him by confessing my sins and my need for Him, I will have the assurance of an eternal fellowship with God. As I came to this realization, tears were already running down my eyes before they made the "altar call," which is a call for action. This is your opportunity, your chance to come forward with gratitude. I said, "Wow, I do not have what these people are talking about. I need Jesus Christ in my life."

That was the beginning. And after the congregation prayed for all of us, they asked us to talk to some counselors who also prayed for me individually. There were so many thoughts going through my mind, and I felt awakened on the inside. That was the beginning of my relationship with the Lord Jesus Christ.

K. C. Armstrong: What an incredible story! Your childhood sounds happy and stable and your religious awakening empowering. But I know that you do a lot of work today helping people who have experienced trauma in their lives. You yourself experienced great trauma at around this time in your life, and at the hands of a family member. Could you tell us about that?

Dr. Feyi Obamehinti: Yes, K. C. At age sixteen, my life changed dramatically when I met my biological mother. It was during this brief time I encountered the trauma that would haunt me into adulthood and turned almost deadly for me.

Just after my fifteenth birthday I was informed that my biological mother wanted to meet me. As I told you, until then I thought my grandparents were actually my parents. I was scared but excited at the same time. I looked forward to it and expected the best. But shortly after meeting for the first time, an accusation by my half-brother resulted in my being whipped across the head with a belt buckle by my mother. The beating opened my forehead, and blood splashed everywhere. With blood gushing out of my forehead, I passed out and woke up in the hospital in pain with a bandaged head. I was then told what had happened: I passed out while running to seek help in the corridor of where we lived. I received several stitches, and I wear that scar across my forehead as a reminder even today.

K. C. Armstrong: That must have been horrible for a kid who probably wasn't sure what was going on.

Dr. Feyi Obamehinti: That traumatic encounter tormented me for years, until I began my restorative journey towards inner healing, freedom and wholeness. After I left the hospital, I moved back to my paternal side of the family. I would have three more encounters with my biological mother after that, and one of those encounters involved her actually putting a gun to my head at her mother's home, where she was staying.

K. C. Armstrong: Would you mind if I asked you why this happened? Unbelievable! I certainly hope your paternal grandparents and family on that side stood up for you in some way.

Dr. Feyi Obamehinti: I can answer that from two perspectives, one is spiritual and the other clinical. It happened because there are always demonic forces that war against God's purposes. Similarly, mental illness is a real problem in our culture today. When left untreated, it can lead to extreme expressions. This is the clinical part that requires professional help, clinical therapy, and medications to realign the body's chemical balances. This is a taboo in the culture I grew up in and needs to be addressed spiritually and clinically.

My paternal grandparents felt it was partly their fault for allowing me to visit and then stay with my biological mother when she requested to see me. On my end, after the belt and gun occurrences, I felt confused, angry and hurt. It felt as if I had a big rock inside of me. I remember nights of waking up from nightmares. I could not understand why a mother would want to harm her own child. This is where my faith in Jesus Christ came in. I began asking God lots of questions. His answers would come in many forms: from the Bible, through prayer, and through people.

K. C. Armstrong: How did you handle all this? After being raised by loving grandparents and finding God, the presence of violence and child cruelty must have devastated and also confused you.

Dr. Feyi Obamehinti: My faith anchored me to seek God to an extent that I probably wouldn't have if this family obstacle had not been in my way. The old conflict between both families still exists today. My parents have not spoken to each other in decades. Any attempts to build a bridge between both sides have been met with resistance, outbursts of anger, and silence in some cases. All of this motivated me to surrender the whole situation to God.

K. C. Armstrong: It seems the actions you encountered were beyond abusive and should have been reported. Why did no one go to the authorities?

Dr. Feyi Obamehinti: In the culture I grew up in, there was a code of secrecy surrounding abuse. A young person dares not speak out against an adult family member. Sometimes my fear to confront my mother was made to look like respect for the elderly. I felt I needed to silently carry the trauma that was still raw with pain attached to the memories of the abuse. For me, that was looking in the mirror every morning and seeing the scar on my forehead and reliving that painful evening with someone that was supposed to be my mother. Also, in my culture, reporting such things in those days to legal authorities had no implications.

K. C. Armstrong: How did this experience change your outlook on life?

Dr. Feyi Obamehinti: I am actually grateful for this traumatic experience. One major outlook I have on life has to do with my relationship with my family, my husband and our three daughters. Each is a gift that I thank God for and never take for granted. We have a strong bond that we cherish daily. This bond has been forged through the ups and downs of life. Though our daughters are adults now, we talk at least twice daily, no matter where any of us may be around the world.

Sometimes, we have to become what we never had. For me, that meant being a loving, caring and present mother for our daughters. I was blessed to have paternal grandparents that I learned about life from. They had already raised their own children and embarked on raising me late in their lives. The experience gave me a deep appreciation for family values and taking responsibility, and I am so grateful to them for that.

K. C. Armstrong: What are your thoughts now about trauma? I'm sure you weren't alone in being expected to keep what happened to you secret for fear of exposing violence and mental illness in your family. This is a heavy emotional burden to carry.

Dr. Feyi Obamehinti: Yes. Trauma is defined basically as an emotional response to tragic things that have happened in our life. Some of the characteristics are acting out or shutting down emotionally. Sometimes trauma also shows up as looking for something, like drugs, alcohol or excessively trying to please, to medicate the internal pain that one is going through. After going through my own trauma, I decided to use what I'd learned to help others deal with it in their own lives.

K. C. Armstrong: I see. You know what's incredible about you? You took these horrible events, and somehow you turned them into a lesson in forgiveness and personal responsibility. We talk on WMAP quite a bit about the power of forgiveness. You have addressed this in your ministry, TV programs and books. Such an important quality for us, but why is it so hard sometimes?

Dr. Feyi Obamehinti: K. C. I would say that when you are bitter and angry, that person who hurt you is actually living inside of you. Practicing forgiveness has empowered me to release people to God, no matter how they might have hurt me. Without forgiveness, you're watching this nightmare, like a movie of your life, over and over again, hurting yourself even more. Experiencing freedom from torments caused by trauma requires freeing the person or persons that have caused us the greatest pain in our lives. This may sound unfair. However, holding on to the memory of any traumatic experience only causes more pain.

Breaking the cycle requires the help of God to release the person or persons and all the components surrounding the traumatic event. As humans, forgiveness is not natural; it takes divine strength to make the choice to let go. Our human nature is set to revenge. This is why the Bible states in Romans 12:19 in the *New Living Translation,* "...never take

> *I am grateful for the trauma—it ushered me to a meaningful and purposeful life.*

revenge. Leave that to the righteous anger of God. For the Scriptures say, 'I will take revenge, I will pay them back,' says the LORD." Simply put, if we have faith in God, we must trust that He can take care of our pains and hurts in a way that will bring honor and glory to Him. Again, this is where understanding the Sovereignty of God comes in. You know you have forgiven the person in question when there is no longer any pain or desire for harm towards that person. A change happens in the soul. Where there was once torment, there now resides a gushing stream of joy, peace and contentment. Forgiveness is a gift to yourself. Then you are at a point where you can actually begin to pray for that person because you realize that if they were actually in their right mind, they wouldn't have done what they did.

Another strategy that I learned and used to be a better person is unlocking the fountain of gratitude. There are so many things to be grateful for, even arising from traumatic experiences. Inner peace is a big one. Those that know the impact of torment know firsthand how it rakes the soul of any sunshine. To wake up to inner peace is something to be grateful for daily. Faith also calls for gratitude. Faith anchors the soul to the Creator. This anchor gives hope to the soul that you are known, seen and loved by a God who holds everything together and is in control of situations beyond human understanding. The icing is loving every bit of one's life, the good and the bad.

Part of this gratitude brought me to accept me for who I am. This is the most powerful validation we can have. This means I am enough because of the love of God for me. It means, I enjoy my own company. This sense of gratitude is a powerful way of living which has allowed me to appreciate my part in this symphony of life. Faith taught me how the power of gratitude helps paint the walls of my soul with beauty. There is an endless song of gratitude that my soul sings. What a beautiful place to be! I am grateful for the trauma—it ushered me to a meaningful and purposeful life.

K. C. Armstrong: That is an amazing reflection on your story and an invaluable example of using all life's experiences to reach our potential. There is so much we can all learn from you! Tell us how your books and TV programs help spread your message of forgiveness, gratitude and faith.

Dr. Feyi Obamehinti: Taking what I have discovered, I have been able to help people find hope and point them in the direction that will accelerate their healing, freedom and restoration. I do this through speaking engagements, virtual coaching, our non-profit organization *Oasis Focus Incorporated* and our Christian TV program *Oasis Connection,* which I co-host with my husband on various networks. We used the name *Oasis* with the idea of a place that supplies life-giving water, or in our case, hope. I would love to do more because I know the need for hope is huge in our culture today, and the time is limited for people to find hope.

K. C. Armstrong: Right. Great name, by the way! What does the *Oasis Focus Organization* do?

Dr. Feyi Obamehinti: Well, first we have the *Marketplace Ministry* which brings free seminars and workshops into disadvantaged communities. We try to share what it means to be a part of that community and contribute to it. For example, one of our sessions talks about *ethical leadership*. To be a leader you have to be yourself, and you are actually a servant, privileged to help people and to do that in a way that brings glory to God.

For the families, we normally have *Parenting Academies*, and we do that by recruiting parents from different community events that we go to. During those events, people normally come to us in our booths to sign up, and we do that in different locations in the north Texas area. We communicate with the people who sign up directly, and we walk them through our programs. Many of them are immigrants that have been here legally but are still trying to find their way— their way to belonging, their way of paving their road to success. They are here, but they don't have any support whatsoever. They don't know what kind of school their kids need to go to, where to obtain a driver's license, or how to get their first home. They don't even know what credit is, even though it's a big part of the American lifestyle. Basically, we walk them through what it means to live here in America physically and what an American life looks like for them.

Our *Public School* aspect falls into two areas, the first one for the student and the second for the educator. We have what we call the *Excellence in Character Scholarship Program* to reach out to our low income graduating seniors. We know how very hard it can be for those students to get money to take care of essentials, money that doesn't go towards tuition or room and board. Rather, this scholarship is for them to spend anyway they want, like for new shoes, new clothes, or underwear.

As part of the application, we ask the students to write an essay describing a specific moment in their life, either a volunteer service or a time that has defined them, maybe something they've overcome. We make our selections looking at all the requirements they've turned in, like the essays, transcripts, and their parents' income tax returns to make sure that they meet all the requirements according to the Federal Government low income criteria and all that. We put that information about our scholarship program on our website, by the way. So that's for the students.

In the second school aspect, we cater to educators that work with students in our public schools. We've had a lot of members volunteer as mentors or coaches, and then we also partner with different school entities. One of the things that has been at our heart has been a passion to help equip and empower educators. Last year we created a Bible study curriculum that will empower educators because a lot of our Advisory Board members have firsthand experience as public school teachers. Teaching is not an easy profession, and the lunchtime Bible study is for staff to get together with colleagues as they eat in fellowship around the word of God. That program was just released last week and we're really excited about it. It's something to put into the hands of teachers as they begin a new school year.

So those are the three major entities, *Parenting Academics, Excellence in Character Scholarship Program*, and the *Bible Study Curriculum*. Then, of course, we have *Oasis Connection* which is a TV program which covers all three areas in reaching out to people with the message of hope and restoration.

K. C. Armstrong: That's certainly a full program affecting a lot of people. You've written many helpful books, as well—some academic and some more personal—to help people in their lives and to bring them closer to the Scriptures. Dr. Obamehinti, thank you for taking us on your journey from Arizona to Nigeria and back again and also on your amazing progression from innocence to abuse and finally to grace, forgiveness and inspiration to others!

One last request: I'd like to ask for your advice to anyone who is where you were near the beginning of your experiences: a victim of trauma, in your case abuse by your own family.

Dr. Feyi Obamehinti: Well first, K. C. I would like to say that it's a joy to be here with the WMAP team. I love you all. You are doing wonderful things and infusing hope through your show every single day. Everyone needs the hope that lets them know that it's going to be okay, and they can be better.

Second, I would say to a person asking for advice: I am honored if my story in any way has inspired you to live better. I give God that glory because that is the essence of what I live for. My purpose is basically to shine the light on His goodness and the hope He offers us all. I would say don't give negativity a chance in your life because it destroys from the inside and has emotional and spiritual consequences. Also, pick up a copy of the Bible and start reading from Proverbs, which is like listening to your mother talking. Your mother loves you so much, giving you advice about life so you won't have to fall into the trenches and into mistakes that others have made. See this as God's voice talking to you, and you can't go wrong.

K. C. Armstrong: Dr. Feyi Obamehinti. Author, speaker, minister, loving wife and mother. We thank you for your great outpouring of wisdom today and for being one of the *World's Most Amazing Women*.

More information about Feyi:

Website: www.crushed2restored.org
Website: www.oasisfocus.org
Book: *Crushed to Restored: Principles of Restoration from the Book of Nehemiah*

HOLISTIC WELLNESS
AND BREAST HEALTH

an interview with Lola Scarborough

*Lola channeled a lifetime of challenges into a study of
holistic prevention and treatment of breast cancer*

INTRODUCTION:

Lola Scarborough has gotten some pushback for the title of her latest
book, but she told me even more controversial is her idea that you can
naturally monitor and improve your own breast health. Lola wants
to enlighten people to take responsibility for their overall well-being.
Her holistic approach to wellness and healing takes daily tasks and
explains how they could affect your health.

Overall health is Lola's true passion, and dedicating her life to that
is something to admire. Her life experiences as a helper definitely
shaped her lifestyle now. As the oldest of eight kids and coming from

a chaotic childhood, she took on a caregiving role and always tried to improve herself and make any bad situation a better one. After healing herself, she is now able to help heal others, and that's a beautiful thing.

INTERVIEW:

K. C. Armstrong: What's special about my next guest, Lola Scarborough, is that she's a very successful natural health and wellness consultant, yoga teacher, author, healer, and entrepreneur who is helping women and their families in many ways. So guys, with no further ado, it's my honor and my privilege to bring to WMAP Miss Lola Scarborough. Lola, what's going on?

Lola Scarborough: Hi K. C. I'm excited to be here with you and your listeners and can't wait to chat a bit. I'm so excited to be a part of this grand adventure, *Simply Amazing Women*!

K. C. Armstrong: Well, you certainly belong here, Lola. Before we get into your story, I was telling the audience earlier this morning about the conversation that we had about the title of your latest book.

Lola Scarborough: It's a little bit attention grabbing! The title of it is *Fighting For Our Tits*.

K. C. Armstrong: Do you know I can't repeat that on my FM show? Isn't that insane? I can call someone an a-hole, but I can't say the name of your book. It's nonsense. Have you gotten flak over this title?

Lola Scarborough: I've gotten a little bit when I've done some advertising with it. The people who seem to be most distressed are women who have already gone through mastectomies and breast cancer, and it's not really the word *tits* that's offensive to them. It's the idea that

I'm saying that there are some natural and holistic things that you can do to support your breast health and maybe help avoid cancer. It seems to be more a push back against the stance of approaching breast health through general health and fitness rather than through western medical intervention.

That view is unfortunate, because there are definitely things we can do and others we can avoid to help ourselves. I'm not saying, "If you had done this, you wouldn't be sick." That's just not true. Sickness happens. It's part of life. But I am saying that there are things you can do to contribute to a full and healthy life instead of going to God one body part at a time. The whole idea of the book is to take the power of your health back into your own hands and to encourage you to see that you are a vital instrument in your own wellness.

K. C. Armstrong: Gotcha. As always, most people who complain are the ones that don't read what they're rejecting. Wouldn't it be great, Lola, if people wouldn't pass judgment on something that they don't know anything about?

Lola Scarborough: Sure. Life would be so much easier! It's a heavily researched book, combining the latest research with alternative approaches to both preventing and treating disease. The book in general is amazing for your overall health, though it's targeted to breast health in particular. The content ranges from traditional practices to medical astrology, past life regression to herbal remedies. We look at breast health holistically and consider overall healthy practices.

K. C. Armstrong: When does this issue usually affect women? I'm kind of ignorant when it comes to this although I know it's a huge problem. Guys get prostate cancer, but not until later in life. When do women typically first see signs of breast problems?

Lola Scarborough: Unfortunately, it seems that the timelines are getting pushed back further and further. Younger women are developing breast cancer as well as older women; the risk goes up after menopause. But you know, it's my opinion that this is because of a lifetime of not understanding the best way to take care of our bodies. Undeniably, younger women are getting it now more than ever. Statistically, one in eight women will develop breast cancer in her lifetime. That is just a horrible number! Anything that we can do to push that number back towards the zero line would make the quality of life for women everywhere so much better.

K. C. Armstrong: Yeah, and this can sneak up on you. From what I hear, you may believe you are healthy, and then all of a sudden you feel a lump or something like that. Tell us how it starts.

Lola Scarborough: When women do their own self breast exam, a lot of times they catch a problem before the mammogram does. When a mammogram confirms or finds a suspicious spot, a biopsy is performed to see if the area is cancerous or not. There are all different levels of breast cancer. Some are very slow growing and, if you lived to be 150 years old, still wouldn't kill you. But there are others that are very fast moving and deadly. So if the lump is decidedly malignant, then the determination is made of what kind of treatment you need.

K. C. Armstrong: I got you. Have you had anyone close to you affected by this?

Lola Scarborough: I am a healer, so I have worked with many women who have gone through treatment for breast cancer or who have had mastectomies, radiation and chemo. Recently in my healing practice I've had many women come in with breast cancer, and it just breaks my heart. I mean, I'm a woman; I have a daughter; I have many female friends. I realized there have to be some underlying causative factors. If we knew what those were, we could teach ourselves to avoid or mitigate them and stand a greater chance of having great breast health until the day we see the good Lord.

Fighting For Our Tits has a very holistic approach, and anyone can read it and benefit from it to avoid cancers of any kind. The book mentions don'ts, which include not drinking fluorinated water, a culprit in many different kinds of diseases, and it also includes recommendations such as exercising, having a good emotional attitude towards life, having supportive social systems, and performing service for other people. It's been proven that helping others really gives your immune system a boost.

K. C. Armstrong: One thing I find remarkable about you is your passion and your desire to help other people. Everything that you're doing is self-funded. You really put your money where your mouth is, so it's obvious you have this real deep desire to help people. Have you always been that way?

Lola Scarborough: I have. Yeah. I'm the oldest of eight children so I think it's my nature, taking care of people and doing things for them. I help people, coming from circumstances where maybe they're not thriving, to improve their health and happiness. Witnessing the deepening of their spirituality and watching their connection to their belief system improve give my life a focus and a meaning that is hard to describe. It's so enlightening and enlivening.

K. C. Armstrong: It must be, Lola, because you're someone who didn't have it easy. What I read is that you grew up amid poverty and violence. How did you turn hardship into a life of compassion?

Lola Scarborough: Well, my feeling is that each of us has a mission. Being a wonderful gardener, or being a wonderful nurse, or being a wonderful father—we all have a mission that we came here to fulfill. I always felt like my mission was helping people. That was true even in my family as I was growing up. I was always the one who was trying to find a way to make things better, find a way to make something that seemed awful a growth opportunity. I started reading when I was very young and focused intently on personal development books for a long time. I also had the love of a great woman, my grandmother. I wouldn't be alive today without her care. It was she who discovered when I was twelve that, like her, I am a healer. My mother loved me too, though she was troubled. I think these things combined with my sense of a mission to help have put me into the field of work that I do.

K. C. Armstrong: How did you develop self confidence?

Lola Scarborough: I had to learn to care for myself before being able to help anyone else. As I mentioned earlier, I was the eldest of eight children. I think that's where my confidence comes from. I had to handle children, drunks, drug addicts, convicts, sexual predators, and mentally ill adults all my life. I handled many of the day-to-day aspects of life in the home. I was able to cook, clean, and take care of children by the time I was eight years old. I also had to take care of myself—no one else was going to do it for me. Plus, I had the added advantage of being a quick learner and, because adults found me to be pretty, it was easier to get them to warm up to me.

These were some additional advantages that I had which some of my siblings were not born with. I also had my grandmother in the background my entire young life, and she rooted for me and bolstered my self-esteem just by loving me the way she did. I believe the accumulation of all of these facets in the early stages gave me a strong sense of self-sufficiency and provided the underpinnings to the leadership qualities I developed later in life.

K. C. Armstrong: Where did your journey begin? Down South, right?

Lola Scarborough: I was actually born in Miami, Florida. We got to the real South when I was ten or so. My mother was an alcoholic; I have no memories of a "sober" mother. She was often violent towards me. We were extremely poor and lived on welfare, although my mother did work. In the early years she worked as a waitress and/ or barmaid, and in her later years she cleaned condos.

My life with her was marked by chaos and drama. By the time I was ten, she had been married four times. Over the course of birth to nine years old, I lived on and off with other relatives, including my aunt, a heroin addict, and my grandmother. Because I was so young, I don't clearly remember, but I must've changed schools fifteen or more times between kindergarten and the sixth grade. When I was almost ten, we moved way out into the country to a place called New Hope, Florida, which took the entire family to a whole new level of misery, poverty, and violence.

New Hope, indeed! Such a misnomer! We all called it "No Hope" Florida. It was a super poverty-stricken place in the South. We didn't have electricity or running water. Food and the basic necessities of life were very scarce. We used to steal rolls of toilet paper from the school, which we used not only for obvious reasons, but also to create pads when we were on our menstrual cycles. We went without shoes and coats in the winter—and it would get really cold where we lived.

K. C. Armstrong: Tell us more about the early years of your life.

Lola Scarborough: I've spoken of my mother, so I'd like to give some background about the father I never had. Although I bear the surname Scarborough, it doesn't genetically belong to me. It belonged to a twenty year old man who was in prison at the time I was born. He was my mother's first husband and his name was Gene. Gene was in the Navy and home on leave in 1958 or so. He and two other Caucasian boys went to Texas Southern College one night to party. Things must've gotten out of control. Charges were brought, and the three men were found guilty of raping an African-American woman at the college. It was a time of high racial tension and my family received death threats, so they moved from Houston to Miami, which is where I was born.

Anyhow, when I was a very young girl my mother would drive back to Houston and take me to the prison to visit Gene. Even though he knew I wasn't biologically his child, he treated me as though I were. My mother told me that the inmates made a big fuss over me, and I really liked them and loved going for the prison visits. I don't remember those visits because I was too young. I think my mother divorced Gene when I was three or four years old and he was still in jail.

My natural father's name was Norman, but I never even met him until I was twenty-nine years old. One day I realized that I would probably be having kids sometime soon, so I thought I should check him out. He had only two fingers on one of his hands, and my mother told me she wasn't sure whether that was because of an accident or a result of a birth defect caused by drugs. So I wrote to him asking to meet, just to see if what happened to him was something that could be passed on to my future children. We met and we have a courteous but cool relationship. The first thing I said when I met him was, "Oh please, please, please don't be an alcoholic, too." But he was.

K. C. Armstrong: I love your honesty.

Lola Scarborough: Well, K.C., I struggled literally from the very beginning. I was born in 1959, and at that time women in childbirth were often given a drug that completely erased the memory of childbirth. This was called *twilight sleep* and was achieved with the administration of a combination of morphine and scopolamine. Even though the women were tied down, thrashing and screaming, they awoke to no memory of the experience so thought they had simply slept through the entire birthing process. My mother was given this twilight sleep, and when she woke up, of course, she didn't remember having me. The nurses presented me to her and she said, "Oh take her away! She's not my baby. I haven't had a baby!" Remember, she was barely seventeen at the time. She refused to believe I was her child.

Finally, they must've convinced her; she took me home and tied some booties on my feet. After a few weeks, because I wouldn't stop crying, she took me back to the doctor. Apparently she had tied the booties so tight that they had cut through all of the flesh on one leg, and I almost lost my foot. Thankfully, I didn't. However, I do have a nice big scar that reminds me every time I look down at my toes to be very, very grateful. Before long she got pregnant again, this time with my sister Barbara, who is no longer with us.

K. C. Armstrong: Barbara was just a little younger than yourself. Could you tell us about her?

Lola Scarborough: My sister Barbara was murdered—I guess it was almost twenty-five years ago. She was hitchhiking to see her boyfriend, Dean, who my mother and brother had stabbed in a fight earlier that day. Dean was in critical care. But Barbara never returned, and it took almost twelve years to find her body because police weren't motivated to look for her. They never did learn who killed her, but she was murdered by a fatal blow to the head. You know, my family had a really interesting reputation in the area that we came from. We were considered to be what is called *poor white trash*. Plus, my family is really reactive. They'd had shootouts with the police, all kinds of stuff.

K. C. Armstrong: I'm so sorry, Lola. Earlier in the interview you said your mother married four times. What about the other husbands?.

Lola Scarborough: After leaving Gene when I was around three, my mother's second husband was a man who had hatcheted his cheating wife and her lover to pieces in their bed. My mother married him right out of prison. The third husband was an Indian man named Big Joe. He was my sister Rachel's daddy. Big Joe was 6'3 or 4, and he and my mother would get into huge fist fights. One time they really got into it, and she went after him with a butcher knife. He locked himself in the car, and she slashed all his tires and smashed the windshield in with a baseball bat. That was just the way it went. Fist fights, knives, everything in the house would get busted up.

My mother was pretty feisty but also extremely intelligent. She only went through the seventh or eighth grade, but she read a lot and had such a mixture of qualities. I mean, she'd be sitting with a Raleigh cigarette hanging out of her mouth and an Old Milwaukee in her left hand talking about how all the prepackaged food in the stores was going to kill us and that in order to stay healthy you need good fresh vegetables from your garden. She was a total character and I loved her. But she had serious issues with violence and rage and alcoholism. Her final husband, with whom she had her last three children, was Bootsie. With each husband, things just kept getting worse.

K. C. Armstrong: I can't imagine all this happening to one person, Lola. As tragic as these marriages must have been for your mother, you were only a little girl learning about the world. It is a miracle that you were able to keep your sanity, much less a feeling of hope for your future. At what point did you start really thinking about a better life?

Lola Scarborough: Well, I finished high school when I was sixteen because I had started early, and also because my grades were so good. By this time my goal was just to get out of my environment alive. Violence was everywhere in my life. My mother and her husbands fought often and fought violently, and I never knew when I was going to become a moving target myself. Mostly they destroyed each other and everything in the home. I felt so unsafe; it was akin to living in a war-charged environment. Food was an issue as well; its appearance on the table was always uncertain.

So, at sixteen I left home for the Atlanta College of Medical, Dental and Business on a scholarship. I lived with a family in Atlanta and took care of their children in return for room and board. At the school, I had an English and business law teacher who told me, "You know, Lola, you're smart, but no one's going to hire you with an accent like that. You sound like a hick from the sticks." Of course, that's exactly what I was. I didn't even realize, though, that I was speaking with what people considered an ignorant-sounding accent. Like they say, a fish doesn't know he's in water, right? I had lived on the Florida-Alabama line and later moved to Georgia. People I was around said *cain't, ort to, hadn't-a...*

K. C. Armstrong: *Fixin?* I remember that from my Kentucky days.

Lola Scarborough: *Fixin,* too.

K. C. Armstrong: That teacher may have been abrasive, but she seems to have taken an interest in you and guided you in doing the hard work that took you further on your journey.

Lola Scarborough: Yes, this teacher helped me a lot. She gave me a tape recorder, and she said, "Just record yourself and listen." So that's what I would do—just talk to myself, and listen to my accent and grammatical errors. There are so many barriers when you're poor and you come from an uneducated family. It's not just a matter of "pulling yourself up by your bootstraps"; a lot of times it's about socializing yourself and learning how to speak and how to present yourself.

K. C. Armstrong: Yeah, you didn't have the best examples. You said that the highest level of education you grew up around was seventh grade. From the start you didn't even have the money for school supplies. The help just wasn't there.

Lola Scarborough: It wasn't there, and I was blind as a bat to boot so I could never see the blackboard, but I was the first person in my family to ever graduate from high school. I am the only person to have a higher degree. After me a couple of my brothers and sisters graduated from high school, and I was really proud of them. A few of them have even taken some college courses which is pretty amazing considering our background. We all went to school sometimes, and the social workers would come around when we missed too much. They came around anyway because we were on food stamps and because of all the violence, alcohol, and poverty in our family.

K. C. Armstrong: At one point you and your brothers and sisters were living on a big farm. What was that like?

Lola Scarborough: We had a sheep and a goat, and they both thought they were dogs. My mother would pick up all these wounded animals and we wound up having seven or eight different kinds of dogs, horses, rabbits and chickens. We had one cow for a little while. Let's see, what else? Oh my goodness. We had all kinds of animals!

K. C. Armstrong: Were they there for slaughter or other reasons?

Lola Scarborough: Again, there was that interesting dichotomy of who my mother was. For example, we had a bunch of rabbits that we'd go out and pet. She'd tell us how we had to take care of them, and how they couldn't take care of themselves, and it would be like "nice rabbit, nice rabbit, nice rabbit, and the next day she'd go out, pick one up by its ears, and that was the end of it. We had a saying, "If it died, it fried." So no way. By the time I was eighteen I was a vegetarian because I'd had my hands in so many guts, and I'd heard too many animals screaming as they died. I had been upfront and close with them with personal contact, so it was emotional.

K. C. Armstrong: That seems almost sociopathic to allow your kids to develop a caring relationship with those animals and then kill them for food.

Lola Scarborough: We never had to kill anything ourselves, but we were there when they did it. We had to do the cleaning and the cooking. That's just what you did in the country. Everyone on all of the other farms did it too. They all killed and butchered and cleaned their own meat.

K. C. Armstrong: I'm sure there was a part of you that enjoyed taking care of these animals because really nobody was taking care of you.

Lola Scarborough: Well, animals are kinder and gentler and a lot more straightforward than people. People are complex. They want to be good and they want to love with all their heart. But something holds people back, while animals don't have that barrier.

K. C. Armstrong: Lola, you talked about finally leaving home to study at a medical, dental and business school in Atlanta. This is where you met the English teacher who took an interest and helped you work on social and speaking skills. Did life improve for you at this point?

Lola Scarborough: When I finished my school program I married the guy that I was dating. I had worked in his daddy's tobacco field when I was fifteen, and that's where I met him. But the marriage only lasted a year. He wasn't an alcoholic, but he did go out and drink sometimes. Mainly he had some mental illness going on. He used to threaten to kill me and kill himself and kill his boss' secretary. I would wake up and he'd be choking me—it wasn't a good scene. It wasn't like that when we were dating, but when we got married, something shifted.

K. C. Armstrong: Lola, can you explain to us a little more about what led you to your work, not only with breast cancer, but with being so devoted to the well-being of others? Your own survival was the issue for so long, and then somehow you redirected that courageous spirit to helping others survive and thrive.

Lola Scarborough: Well I'm a healer, and I work with a lot of women at our yoga studio. As a healer I started noticing a trend about eighteen years ago when more and more women were coming to me because they had breast cancer. They'd gone through chemo, radiation, and mastectomies, and a lot of times all three of those things. I saw some of them die from the treatments.

K. C. Armstrong: How did you make the leap from that observation to the creation of your book?

Lola Scarborough: I'm a bit of a bookworm and a research rat. So for the last eight or nine years I have been digging around in the research about breast cancer, what may trigger it, and what might keep us from developing it. I actually woke up my husband four years ago and told him, "I'm going to write a book." He had some questions, maybe a few doubts, but last year I announced to him, *"I'm ready."*

> *I have been digging around in the research about breast cancer, what may trigger it, and what might keep us from developing it.*

So I sat down, and within three weeks' time I wrote a 250 page book pulling together the research that I'd been doing for all those years, as well as including information about alternative and complementary modalities to keep yourself well. I talk about nutrition. I talk about emotions. I talk about what perfumes, fluoride and other common items do to your body. My inspiration was to put all the pertinent information out there and into the hands of women who can, perhaps, help themselves avoid breast cancer.

K. C. Armstrong: I see. How does your yoga studio fit into your whole profile of healing holistically and self-care?

Lola Scarborough: I'm trained in Ayurveda, a nutritional and life-style system of India and a very deep sister science to yoga. Using those two ideologies and the training that I got as a Spenser-certified life coach, I work with people at all levels on many aspects of their lives: from their diet, to what time they wake up in the morning, to the color of clothing that they wear. I also do energy work with folks, which helps the emotional body relax. So rolling it all together, I'm able to offer people a full package of wellness—mind, body, and spirit.

My husband and I own Yoga Lola Studios, which gives us a forum in which people can rediscover their bodies, express their emotions, and develop their spiritual strength. Through the example we set at the Studio and by how we live our lives—coupled with my books and our teachings—we show people that compassion is the highest embodiment of the divine spark that lives within all of us and that hardships can be overcome.

K. C. Armstrong: What do you tell people who are going through great struggles like yours?

Lola Scarborough: I tell them, "Don't give up, and don't give in. You are enough, and you can make a difference. What appears as a hardship is really a lesson. Use birth control, stay off drugs and alcohol, and remember you are here because the Universe thought that what you had to bring to this Earth was important enough to put you in a body."

K. C. Armstrong: You have pretty much summed up the theme of this entire book and each story it contains! In *Simply Amazing,* my last book, I began with the quote "Adversity is a teaching tool…" It's a tough statement and hard to imply that we should actually welcome the storms we weather in our lives. But people like yourself, who go through intense pain and then emerge strong and confident, best understand the concept of personal growth earned through experience.

Lola Scarborough: Right, K. C. Through my experiences, I've come to believe that I have the Universe on my side and that I can do the impossible. What I came out of and what I made of it were blessings from Grace. They have given me an ongoing sense of gratitude for what I have. I loved my mother, and I would do it all over again. My life with her gave me strength, willpower, compassion, and the ability to forgive what might, to others, seem unforgivable. She also made me independent and largely immune to the pressure to conform. I learned to never give up, even when the odds are not in my favor. The most important thing it did, though, was to cement in me a compelling commitment to serve others. My greatest desire is to become a multi-millionaire and provide clean water, simple nutritious food, and dignity to those whose circumstances do not allow them to help themselves. I want to be the world's Fairy Godmother!

K. C. Armstrong: (Smiles) Lola, you came from an unbelievable background where you suffered poverty, violence, hunger, abuse, and experiences no child should ever see or endure. But through your commitment to heal yourself, you now have the gift to heal, console and inspire others. You own a prosperous yoga and wellness center, have raised two beautiful children with your awesome husband, have written books with more on the way, and have multiple degrees including a PhD in Comparative Religion. You are certainly one of the *World's Most Amazing Women.* No one with the greatest fame or fortune can rival what you have accomplished, and that's what our radio station and series of *Simply Amazing* books want the world to see! Thank you for sharing your story with us today.

More information about Lola:

Website: www.yogalola.com
Book: *Fighting For Our Tits, A Woman's Battle Cry* (Women's Issues)
Book: *Molten Woman, Sins, Sex, Spirit & In-Sanity* (Poetry)

ASCENSION

an interview with Wendy Ann

Wendy Ann learned to channel her free spirit into an expressive opportunity for herself and her group of misfits

INTRODUCTION:

I thought a lot about my talks with Wendy Ann and read her interview transcripts over several times. I felt I was missing something. Wendy Ann is smart, funny and creative, but her story seemed to come back to a thread I couldn't put my finger on. After one more Gatorade, it hit me. What's the opposite of acceptance? JUDGMENT. So I've nicknamed Wendy's chapter "The No-judgement Zone."

Here's a story of a somewhat defiant child who was criticized for acting on her free spirit and creativity. She was judged by authority figures as not fitting into their predetermined categories, but then she went on to learn how to use her independent spirit to bridge differences. Through great teachers and life experiences, Wendy Ann's journey has led her to celebrate human diversity and show, rather than tell, others her view of the world. See if you agree with my assessment as you read Wendy Ann's interview.

INTERVIEW:

K. C. Armstrong: Our next guest, Wendy Ann, was a bit of a renegade as a child. In fact, she recalls her rebellion against authority dating back to at least the age of eight, when her teachers found her third grade writing project "too explicit." Wendy was a regular in the principal's office and was even asked to leave church a few times because she refused to fit into a traditional mold. From the start she was feisty, independent and artistic, and it was an interesting journey for her to learn how to direct that individuality effectively. Welcome, Wendy! We have lots to talk about today!

Wendy Ann: Thank you so much for having me.

K. C. Armstrong: I have to tell you, I just love your attitude about being yourself and not allowing others to squeeze you into some predefined category! That was very brave, especially as an eight year old! You were already writing at that age and have continued ever since, right?

Wendy Ann: Yes, all true. Initially, rebelling did more harm than good. I spent more time in the principal's office than anyone I've ever met. I'd been thrown out of church a handful of times, and I had to contend with years of counseling. But I never lost my benevolence, creativity, or my acceptance of diversity. I was drawn to the oddballs and minorities who, like me, struggled with adversity, bullies, and oppression. All my experiences, even then, just gave me creative fuel.

K. C. Armstrong: It seems your art, in this case writing, was necessary for you to truly express yourself when others were trying to suppress your free-spirited behavior.

Wendy Ann: Yes. Writing has always been a prominent aspect of my life. It was important to me to be able to release my inner monologue, to be able to capture my thoughts, to archive them, to immortalize them, and—most importantly—to *see* them. To harness your thoughts and actually look at them by releasing them onto paper offers a great benefit. The words and ideas become more concrete. Sometimes you write with great thought; other times it's more impulsive writing, like in the case of poetry. You know, you just release it without thinking about rules or about your handwriting or about how it sounds. You just pour it out of your heart.

K. C. Armstrong: Wait! Tell me, Wendy, that you have horrible handwriting! I've always been the guy with the illegible chicken-scratch.

Wendy Ann: My handwriting is so bad, I have friends who can actually make it out better than I do.

K. C. Armstrong: (laughs) Me too. I believe you are releasing a new work of fiction called *Sage* in April or May of this year. Is this something you've been working on for a while?

Wendy Ann: Yes, K. C. *Sage* is actually the first of what will be a four part *Ascension* series. Ascension essentially means *to rise.* It is predominantly about the evolution of sex to love, which is not to say that it isn't about finite to immortal, organic to ether, and movement from the first chakra to the seventh. Primarily though, *Sage* follows the evolution of sex to love, and the second book will be focused on chaos to peace.

And yes, it is something I've been working on a long time. Looking back to 2009, my primary writing project was to create a concept based on mystery, romance, and sensuality. Actually, the writing was pretty dark. I wound up putting it down for nine years while I went through this crazy growth process. During those years I learned so much that when I finally picked the project back up, I added 60,000 more words, and all of them were based on that evolutionary process. I grew and learned, and that is how the book deepened and grew.

K. C. Armstrong: And that is the journey I hope you will take us on. Let's start with a little about your childhood.

Wendy Ann: My childhood was a paradox. I grew up in a rough neighborhood, but I lived in an incredibly enchanting home and made amazing lifelong friends. I was in foster care but was fortunate enough to become adopted by a loving family that allowed close ties with the kinder members of my biological family, including my parents who'd visit regularly. I had severe ADHD, but I was encouraged to take dance and gymnastics and enjoy sports like boxing, climbing, track and field, and also more creative outlets to channel my excessive energy.

I was so blessed to have many amazing people in my life growing up. For instance, Sue, my adoptive mother, was the matriarch of my life and, actually, of many people's lives. My biological mother had been friends with Sue's children, which is how they met years before I was born. Sue took my mother under her wing, and eventually she ended up doing the same for me.

K. C. Armstrong: Your mom must have been very young.

Wendy Ann: Right. My mother and my father are both amazing people. It was a rough decision on their part to give me to foster care, since not only were they so young, but they were also going through a separation when their families didn't get along with one another. It wasn't the best environment for me to be in as a child. So they placed me in Sue's care. She was like a professional mother who attended to many children, both her own and foster children as well.

K. C. Armstrong: How many kids were there in your household?

Wendy Ann: Well, Sue had six of her own biological children and a huge house. When her kids moved out and went to college, she had extra rooms which she used to rescue children—and some stray animals, too! We usually had between five and seven foster kids in the house at a time. Some would stay two weeks; some would stay two months. The longest any of them lived there was about three years.

K. C. Armstrong: Another person who greatly affected your life was your Grandpa Kelley. Tell us about him and his influence.

Wendy Ann: Grandpa Kelley was an inspiration to me, especially because of how selfless he was. You know, there was always a paradox in my life, and whenever I'm in a really dark situation, I seek out the brightest light. Through all of my life, that was Grandpa Kelley. His love for everybody was unconditional. He believed even the most wretched people were only that way because they lacked love. He was also more forgiving and less judgmental than I am. I aspire to be like him.

K. C. Armstrong: You were lucky to have had that incredible example. When he passed away, what did you lose personally?

Wendy Ann: I felt like the whole world lost something great when he passed. What I lost, I feel, was a human being who really did care about people. He was able to accept everybody for who they were. He never judged. And that is something that I strive to be like to this day. It was a lot easier when I had that example in front of me. He was like a coach. I guess I lost my forgiveness coach when I lost him.

K. C. Armstrong: And that's unfortunate, but we all make judgments, as much as we don't want to. It's very hard not to.

Wendy Ann: Grandpa Kelley had mastered the art. He would also spend a great deal of time with people who were abandoned. He was even given a key to the city of Worcester, my hometown, as a result of his unconditional philanthropy and the time that he spent with the sick and dying, particularly those who had nobody. He would seek the loneliest, saddest person who was near their last breath and give them love and care during their last days. I think this was his idea of a gift from God.

K. C. Armstrong: He thought everybody was worth saving. What a wonderful man. How do you think he got to that ascension?

Wendy Ann: You know, his love life started with someone from an entirely different country. Although he was from Ireland and his wife was from the Middle East, they found commonality in their love. I think the loving aspects of the Bible that they both loved and their religion were what inspired them. I'm an eclectic spiritualist and don't profess to be religious. In their cases, though, I think religion inspired a great deal. The unconditional love of Jesus was something that they really believed and implemented. It was sacred to Grandpa Kelley to have an open heart and to accept and forgive and to practice what many Christians—dare I say it—don't.

K. C. Armstrong: Yes. It's easy to talk. As the Bible says, actions reveal someone's true character. Anybody can say the preferred words, but the truth is in what you do. It sounds like Grandpa Kelley transferred that wisdom to you. I see a lot of that in your writing and in your relationships. For example, I know that diversity is extremely important to you. You don't just talk about acceptance, you act on what you say. And this brings us to another great example of positivity you encourage in your life.

Wendy Ann: Yes! By about sixteen, I began to align myself with incredible people who saw through the matrix of conformity and used creative outlets to exploit it as much as I did. Using the internet and the diverse range of people I met by residing/working in two large cities and a few small towns, I began cherry-picking an eclectic range of awesome minds who have become forever members of my lifelong tribe of artistic rebels.

K. C. Armstrong: You refer to these people as your "tribe." What do you mean by that?

Wendy Ann: My *tribe* is made up of twenty-two people like myself who use art as a means to bridge the communication between unique, amazing, like-minded human beings and make an impact on this world. One member is a musician. Others are belly dancers. I deliberately selected all kinds of people, and each one began as a personal friend. But in spite of the eclectic mix, our common need is a creative outlet to function. That need gives us something deep to latch on to, something that has held us together. It's been our adhesive for, in some cases, up to twenty-five years.

K. C. Armstrong: It's so cool that you've found these close relationships through creativity and the need to express and connect. You're not the type that's going to a loud bar and make small talk. That to you is hell, I bet.

Wendy Ann: It is now. I mean, I definitely spent some teenage years feeling differently. Then it was just losing myself in the music and dancing. You're right, though. Small talk is something I've never, ever enjoyed. I'd rather be quiet. I just nod if the conversation is about as deep as a puddle. I can only swim in it for five minutes, if that.

K. C. Armstrong: Tell us more about this interesting and diverse "tribe" of people that are artists in all sorts of different mediums.

Wendy Ann: In our group, we have one member from India, one from Asia, one from the Islands. We have African-Americans, Irish, Hispanics—just about every race. Bisexual, gay, asexual, heterosexual, Christian, atheist, agnostic, eclectic spiritualist, pagan: we all sit together and feel like we've been friends forever. Usually there are between two and five of us at a time with a lot of talking, laughing, and a ton of making fun of each other. Sometimes, in the name of dark humor, it may sound like we're not getting along as we joke with one another! But everything is on the table with us; we don't hold back. We tell each other things that most friends probably don't share, and none of us feels awkward or uncomfortable. We've already addressed the hard part which is that, according to society, we probably shouldn't be getting along at all.

K. C. Armstrong: And how has this tribe affected your writing?

Wendy Ann: Oh, they inspire me. And they humble me too, which is important. Our tribe includes outstanding writers and poets, musicians, lyricists, photographers, rappers—we're just all over the creative spectrum! One writer, lyricist and musician, whose work is pretty dark, spends most of his time rescuing animals. Many of our artists are about helping other people as well as animals.

K. C. Armstrong: It sounds like you surround yourself with people who are not only extremely talented, but who are also not just out for themselves. They really want to make a difference in the world, and they want to help other people.

Wendy Ann: I'm not sure if all of them consciously plan on how they can go out and save the world. It is definitely a part of what they do, though. All of us are the type of people that empathizes with abuse of the innocent—especially animals and children—to the point that it pains us to hear of such things. Our art, especially its darker aspects, derives from the harsh reality of those things, like abuse, that people need to be less complacent with and actually look at. Art can provide a mirror to the truth, thereby diagnosing a problem that needs to be fixed. Whether our ears want to hear it, whether we want to see it, whether we want to experience it or not, it exists. Each and every one of my tribe members, for the sake of honesty, will go there to face truth. Being so diverse, we can do that without hurting each other's feelings or belittling one another. We can actually have the ability to see past the conundrum of superficial man-made factions.

K. C. Armstrong: You explain it very well, and I think we need more of that acceptance and honesty. We can agree on the importance of surrounding ourselves with such positive people. You know, a lot of people seem drawn to negativity.

Wendy Ann: There's another paradox. You can focus on the parts in life that bring you down, or you could focus on the parts that can enlighten you and better you as a human being. There have been times in my life when I have focused in the wrong direction, and it only held me back. It only kept me anchored to negativity and angst and didn't give me anything to aspire for. To let go of that negativity is to cut off the chains of your spiritual evolution. Like most of us, I'm in a process of evolving. You and I have agreed about this recently; don't award Stalin and Hitler your attention when at that same exact time in history, at the turn of the 20th century, you could be rewarding Tesla and Einstein.

K. C. Armstrong: That's that paradox that you talk about? Both good and evil coexist?

Wendy Ann: Exactly. They're both happening at the same time and even the same place. It comes down to what you choose to focus on. I think that we would be in a completely different place as a human collective if we didn't reward bad people with our attention. Of course, what we consider *bad* is subjective, but negative people do like attention. And also conflict, right? Chaos. So if you give that to them, if you award them that, then what's to deter them from continuing in the same way?

K. C. Armstrong: That's really insightful.

Wendy Ann: Well, bad advertising is still advertising, right? You could instead award your attention to those who could actually help humanity or people like yourself who want to evolve. We could look at Martin Luther King, for instance. I absolutely love him. One of my favorite things that he said was to base our opinions on the content of people's character. It's profoundly important.

K. C. Armstrong: It seems like that should be logical to everyone.

Wendy Ann: But it's not. Instead of focusing on the negative, these people could be listening to what you're doing on the *World's Most Amazing People*. On the radio and in your books you're promoting people who have overcome their problems. You're not tearing them down.

K. C. Armstrong: You're right. We need to keep sight of what's possible. It seems that many influential people in your life have added to your growth in different ways. Is this what was brewing during your nine years between dropping your first novel and later picking it up and being able to bring it, 60,000 words later, to completion?

Wendy Ann: Absolutely yes. Surround yourself with positivity.

I also learned as I matured how to channel my independent thinking better. It's simple. I've realized that people who attempt to change someone else actually degrade that person. Everyone has her own subjective vision of life. To try to tell somebody that their perspective is entirely wrong is a lot different than letting them see who you are and giving them something that they may or may not like, instead of deflecting. You are opening up a part of yourself that doesn't cause their defense mechanism to rise. It's certainly more difficult to have an amicable conversation when you're trying to boss somebody around.

But the point that I'm trying to make is that none of us are perfect. I think a lot of the problem with society right now is that we focus on each other's imperfections instead of the good messages that we're trying to sell. We can't force our ways onto others. It's so easy to be critical and say, "She's all about protecting

> *Your expression comes from a place of experience— something you've heard, something that's inspired you, something that's hurt you.*

the planet. But look, she uses plastic straws." I do use paper straws, don't get me wrong, and I do avoid red meat. But I'm still eating poultry and I'm still eating fish. So, you know, somebody who is vegan can look at me and say that I'm not a true animal lover because I'm not at their level yet.

We are all at different levels and have completely different things to offer. Like we were discussing earlier, if instead of trying to convert people you inspire them, you'll have more success. Instead of saying, "Hey, you're going to hell because you're eating meat," you can say, "Hey, try these meatballs. They're meatless, and they're great!"

K. C. Armstrong: That's definitely a better way to go about it.

Wendy Ann: Keep in mind that the hierarchy of society has used divide-and-conquer techniques to keep human beings under control for millennia. And that will continue to work as long as we try to force people to see things our way instead of organically and gracefully teaching them who we are. I learned that the world needed more amicable mediation and less preachy litigation. I noticed that inspiring people was more beneficial than trying to convert them.

K. C. Armstrong: What else?

Wendy Ann: Don't turn your nose up at people who aren't at your same stage in the evolution process. I look at who I was—sometimes a day ago or a year ago, but especially five or ten years ago. I realize that you should take the good things with you and you learn from the bad things; you can decide which of those you want to shape you. You're the sculptor of your own life. You really do learn that hands-on with art. Creativity doesn't derive from nothing. It comes from inside you somehow, whether it's a poem, a painting, a sculpture, a lecture—whichever form you use. Your expression comes from a place of experience— something you've heard, something that's inspired you, something that's hurt you. You have the ability to transform that. A lot of people don't do that. They recycle other people's ideas.

K. C. Armstrong: Exactly. And never implement their own.

Wendy Ann: Like skimming over a painting just for the sake of saying that you looked at it, as opposed to being mesmerized by it. I think a lot of people skim over life in that same way instead of really immersing themselves in it.

K. C. Armstrong: That's so accurate. It sounds like you are the same creative open-minded person you were as a young girl, but you have become wise in your interactions with others. You were so fortunate to have the love and guidance of your parents, your adoptive mother, your Grandpa Kelley and your "tribe," but you did the hard work of identifying and rooting out unnecessary negativity and judgment in your life. I know the loss of your adoptive mother, Sue, and your Grandpa Kelley were devastating to you. Were their passings also a part of your evolution?

Wendy Ann: Yes, of course. I have such gratitude for the love in my life. I appreciate all that I do have now because you never know when you're going to lose it. Everything is finite.

K. C. Armstrong: And now you're helping other people with this message of gratitude, mutual respect, and focus on the positive. I love the term that you use: *ascension*, and I can't wait to see how all of this wisdom reveals itself in *Sage* and your entire four book series. What last thoughts would you like to leave with our listeners and readers?

Wendy Ann: First, it's amazing to be part of this series, and I feel you're doing exactly what I try to do. You're promoting people who've overcome problems, and you're inspiring people instead of criticizing them. So on that notion I would like to reiterate that none of us are perfect and that life is a growing process. We all make mistakes, but we can honor our hearts and do our best to protect the innocent.

I'd also like to bring attention to the concepts of overcoming adversity through positive causes and art, and to cheering on empathy. I've come to appreciate freedom and peace of mind in a more profound way than ever before, and I try my best not to squander my time on things that do not better myself or the world in some way. That especially includes my favorite pastime-writing.

K. C. Armstrong: Wendy, you've said some really amazing things that people needed to hear today. So I thank you for being a part of this project, and for just for being who you are, one of the *World's Most Amazing Women.*

More information about Wendy Ann:

Website: www.roguepoet.net

BALANCE AND PEACE

an interview with Lotus Prana Zheng

*After a bout of depression, Lotus decided to heal
herself so she could help others do the same*

INTRODUCTION:

Lotus Prana Zheng is an alternative therapist, Reiki master, and
I-Ching consultant. After early disappointments and depression,
Lotus was at a crossroads in her life. She decided to read up on ancient
texts, which contained information about energy healing methods
and psychology, to get to the bottom of what she was feeling. After
honing these methods that helped her relieve her own depression,
she took a step back and thought about those who might be suffering
from depression as she had.

Lotus shows that she's willing to put the work in to help other troubled souls by the number of people she's aided and her willingness
to travel around the world to target those who need her the most.

She has a deep insight into the subject of depression, and her unconventional methods have guided many in successfully getting past the traumas in their lives.

INTERVIEW:

K. C. Armstrong: All right guys. Our next guest found her calling at probably the lowest point in her life. Thankfully, she was able to follow that realization to help others going through the deep depression that she herself has experienced. Lotus Zheng has actually developed a new type of therapy which is helping many people improve their lives. So let's welcome Lotus to the show to tell us more about how she has been able to use her background to uplift others. Lotus, welcome to the show.

Lotus Zheng: Hi, K.C. Thank you for having me here. I have been so busy, but I have been looking forward to this talk with you.

K. C. Armstrong: Thank you for making time for our interview today, Lotus. You come to us all the way from China, right?

Lotus Zheng: I live in Seattle, Washington now. But I was born in Northern China in 1971. I moved to the U.S. in 2007 from Shanghai.

K. C. Armstrong: What was your life like there?

Lotus Zheng: Well, my childhood was lonely. When I was little I used to lie down on a bamboo mat outside in the summertime. I have one very vivid memory of looking up at the vast night sky and feeling a strong pull to one corner of it. It seemed something was pulling me upward in that direction. I don't know how to describe it, but I was afraid that I would be lifted into that piece of the sky. I don't know if that fear was from an isolation I felt or simply the result of a rich imagination.

But either way, I was a weird kid. In elementary school I spent lots of time in the library and the bookstore reading books about philosophy-Western philosophy mostly. Oh, and also stories about aliens. I was drawn to alien stories, maybe because of the attraction I felt from the sky.

Actually, I had an actual experience with a UFO which I didn't discuss for my entire childhood since I thought no one would believe me.

K. C. Armstrong: No way!

Lotus Zheng: Yes! And I have to say it was very scary. When I was thirteen years old I was in middle school and living in a school dorm. One night, I was looking out a window and saw a huge UFO floating near the window. It looked like one big plate on top of another. And then I disappeared from the dorm, and I don't know when or how I went back. Once I realized I was back in my dorm room, I was confused and afraid. Did I have a dream? It felt so real. Where did I go? I didn't remember anything except that plate-shaped UFO and sort of "waking up" back in my room.

The next morning I wanted to tell my roommates, but I held back because I was worried that they would laugh at me. I carried that secret until thirty years later, in July of 2015, when I went to a UFO Conference where I learned that many people had similar experiences. So I began seeing hypno-therapists to try to get that lost piece of my memory back. The problem is, every time I would try to enter into a trance, I'd block myself within the first few minutes. I guess my fears got in the way of allowing myself to be hypnotized. I was worried I might get some scary memories back. I'm still not sure if this was a dream or if it was for real.

Then, when I was in high school, some students and I were picked to be in a study called "Qigong Improves Intelligence," which was run by the Institute of Aerospace Medical Engineering. Qigong, not so well-known in the West, is a system of coordinated body movements, breathing and meditation used widely in the East to promote spirituality and health. The study suggested that Qigong, rooted in philosophy, martial arts, and Chinese medicine, can actually improve intelligence. All of us who participated in the study felt our brains worked much faster, and we also felt a big improvement in physical health. So from that time I concentrated on my Qigong practice, and my body got continually stronger as my brain got sharper. I became more connected to the universe and more spiritual.

K. C. Armstrong: That's pretty incredible. When you were participating in this study and practicing so much spirituality, did your friends look at you differently because you were deeply involved in something they may not have known much about?

> *Was it possible for me to help other people going through the same inner turmoil?*

Lotus Zheng: Honestly, at the beginning, all of them were scared of me! First they thought I was lying; second they thought I was scary and weird. After some time, though, they got curious and we started practicing Qigong together.

K. C. Armstrong: You certainly have an interesting background! At some point, though, you dealt with depression?

Lotus Zheng: Yes. By my early 20's I was really unhappy-working at a bank job that I hated and living with my parents. My life was unsatisfying and disappointing. I got to a point where I didn't even want to go to work. My coworkers were unfriendly, and I had lost my first love, which was devastating. There was no joy at all in my life. I was depressed, and I couldn't see a way out. That's when I had a personal transformation.

K. C. Armstrong: What happened?

Lotus Zheng: I left home and sank deeper into depression. One day I was at the beach, and I felt I really didn't want to live anymore. I felt so empty and hopeless. I waded into the cold water, but once I was up to my neck in icy water on the verge of taking my own life, I heard a voice: "You are not done yet!"

It suddenly occurred to me that, although I was suffering so badly, countless other people probably were feeling the same way. Maybe I should think about that. Was it possible for me to help other people going through the same inner turmoil? This was such a powerful thought as it took me away from my own selfishness and into a mindset of compassion for others. I knew how they felt, but if I couldn't help myself, how could I help them?

So I left the beach, and I tried to learn everything I could about depression and how to overcome it. I studied psychology and several different energy healing methods and combined them with Qigong and *I Ching*, a two and a half thousand year old ancient divination text which is read throughout the world. *I Ching* comments on religion, psychoanalysis, art, and much more.

K. C. Armstrong: You studied ancient texts and healing methods to cure yourself first. Were you able to do that without help?

Lotus Zheng: I didn't get any professional help, but I did wind up combining psychology and holistic treatments to eventually overcome my depression. Through my feelings of hopelessness, I realized how important mental health is for all people. That sinking feeling of desperation shouldn't have to be dealt with alone. I began reaching out to people who had similar issues and taught them some techniques that had worked for me. And that's how I found my life purpose: helping other people overcome depression and other mental issues and assist them in reaching their high potentials.

K. C. Armstrong: All this happened while you were still living in China?

Lotus Zheng: Yes. I began my practice in Shanghai, but in 2007 I moved to the U.S. for more freedom and opportunities. Right now I have a company in Seattle called Lotus Prana LLC, which is devoted to overcoming depression, anxiety, phobias, traumas, PTSD, and addictions while building confidence, positive patterns, good relationships, and spiritual growth.

K. C. Armstrong: When you began your practice in China, you were just getting over major depression yourself. Did you find it difficult to transition from your previous job in banking into this kind of work while you were still recovering from your own problem?

Lotus Zheng: It didn't feel difficult because I would share my depression experience with my clients first, before they told me what was happening with them. No. It was easy to open up to them and for them to open themselves to me. After all, we could understand each other's feelings.

K. C. Armstrong: Maybe you can tell us about some of the interactions you've had with your clients.

Lotus Zheng: Oh yes! I especially want to mention one young lady in her early twenties who came to my office. She suffered from serious depression and anxiety and had been in an abusive relationship. When she came in, we looked for root causes of those issues by discussing her childhood. This is where most mental health issues come from.

After the very first session she felt extremely blissful and super confident, and she became very encouraged when a wound on her hand was unexpectedly healed. She was amazed at that and developed a new, brighter outlook. Although this woman had never sung in public before, after several sessions she started to write and sing her own songs and put her recordings on YouTube! She had never taken an interest in drawing, but she began to do a good job in painting, and I received one of her works as a beautiful reminder of her progress.

This woman got over her abusive relationship with her ex, and her relationship with her parents improved. After her sessions, her *third eye* opened to receive wisdom and insight. She could see things before they actually happened. After several appointments, she moved back to her hometown to be with her family, but we still keep in touch. When she first came to me she was waitressing in a bar, but now she is teaching high school kids in low income neighborhoods. She now has a healthy, happy and fulfilling life helping people and creating her art. After going back to school to get a master's degree in psychology, she will be taking my training to be a therapist. Before she left, she said to me, "Lotus, you completely changed my life. I want to be a person like you to help others as you are doing." I was really touched, especially since her sessions brought out amazing psychic abilities.

K. C. Armstrong: That's a remarkable change! And that young woman's gratitude must give you a great feeling and more confidence in your own abilities. When did you decide that you wanted to write, and what was your inspiration?

Lotus Zheng: I started writing because my clients convinced me that I could inspire far more people that way. They even said I could use their stories in the book, if that would help others going through similar problems.

K. C. Armstrong: Lotus, we've heard about your journey from China to the US, but let's focus right now on your biggest accomplishments. I know that, as well as authoring two books, you are the creator of a new type of therapy called *Lotus Prana Quantum Therapy.* I'm sure that is an accumulation of all your experience, study and spiritual practice. Can you tell us more about that?

Lotus Zheng: Sure. As I mentioned earlier, my clients actually suggested I share information about this new therapy in book form for wider awareness. They kindly allowed me to describe their therapy sessions, of course not under their real names, but all completely factual. The book almost reads like a novel, because each story is unique and personal. Through it, a reader can get a good idea of what is possible in the therapy and what the sessions are like.

I explain step by step how this new therapy is applied, in thirty-four real cases, to overcome depression, anxiety, traumas, addictions, PTSD, negative patterns, and negative emotions, and to improve self-esteem, self-image, relationships, career, sexual performance and much more.

The first steps involve finding a client's root causes of depression or other issues. It is not enough to cover the symptom, like with medication. You must go back to the old memories and remove the root of the traumas by resolving childhood issues and removing old patterns from your past. We need to do energy work to balance energy in all chakras and store positive data, images, and emotions in your energy system. When your energy is balanced, you feel at peace. Qigong is an important part of the technique, as it promotes both spiritual and physical health. When we do this deep work with your past experiences which have created blocked energy and negative impulses today, we sometimes can even experience visions of past and future lives.

Lotus Prana Quantum Therapy combines holistic counseling with elements of psychology, inner child therapy, reiki healing, guided meditation, Qigong and more Chinese and holistic energy healing techniques. These may include Egyptian Seichim healing, DNA memory repairing, Chinese I Ching & Bagua, Yin Yang balancing and aura cleansing, inner parents healing, and other methods. It is so precise that I have patents pending in the U.S. and overseas. You can see how all my background led to this. I have had such great results in helping people find balance, peace, love, happiness, success and fulfillment in their lives.

K. C. Armstrong: That's what we strive for, Lotus: to use our challenges to ease the way for others. You are a great example of that. You mentioned meditation. Is that an important part of your therapy?

Lotus Zheng: Yes, K. C. Meditation is both calming and energizing! It quiets your mind and helps you to focus on what you need to do, either throughout the day, or for the health of your mind. I help many clients develop self-love and confidence through even just a five minute daily meditation. For example, for just that amount of time we can talk to our inner children: "How are you today? I love you and I'm proud of you. You did well today." Speak kindly to yourself. Remember, energy attracts like energy. With good energy, all good things will come.

K. C. Armstrong: Great advice, Lotus.

Lotus Zheng: Thank you! Once my therapy model is patented I hope to spend much of my time in training others to use it effectively so we can get that many more people to connect with their higher selves, gaining a peaceful mind, happiness, and health.

At the end of the book I give my idea of what the earth and humans might be like in three thousand years. This observation is based on the visions that my clients saw during the therapy sessions when their psychic abilities were expanded.

K. C. Armstrong: Lotus, does everyone have a gift to have these visions, or is it something you need to learn? Can all your clients expect to have these visions of the future?

Lotus Zheng: K.C., I believe that everybody has the potential, but it only works when people are open to it.

K. C. Armstrong: Isn't it amazing that all this came from that incident at the beach when you thought, for that moment in time, that your life was not worth living? Through understanding your own depression, much research and dedication, you have been able to design a wide-ranging method to effectively route out depression and other painful mindsets. That is so remarkable. What would you like to tell our listeners and readers, looking back on your whole journey?

Lotus Zheng: First of all, I learned that success for me is not found in other people's eyes or to please my parents. It is to be true to myself, to do what I love and what I am good at, to enjoy every moment of life, and help people with their self improvement in the way that I can. I found my real passion for life and after many years of doing my work, I still feel lucky and happy everyday to do what I love and to help people improve their lives.

I'd like to tell your listeners and readers who may be depressed that I was there before. I understand how you feel, what you go through, and where you are emotionally. I overcame my issues, and I am very happy now. I believe you can do the same thing! Be who you are, do what you love, help people using the talents that you have developed. We all have experiences and skills that can be used to help others which will also help ourselves just as much.

K. C. Armstrong: Thank you, Lotus. You are a fascinating person with good stories, a sense of humor, and also wisdom we can learn from. This is why we appreciate you for being one of the *World's Most Amazing Women!*

More information about Lotus:

Website: http://www.lotusprana.org/ (Lotus Prana Energy Living)
Website: http://www.lotusprana.com/ (and .net-LotusPrana LLC)
Book: *Play The Magic of Life Transformation: New Human On New Earth*

CHOOSING LIFE

an interview with Misti Rains

Misti reminds us to stay present and not take our days for granted

INTRODUCTION:

Misti Rains has the most amazing outlook on life. She was told she was going to die and considered giving up hope for life. Through her health crisis, however, she found peace in her life with the realization that every situation is a learning opportunity for individual growth. Misti actually declared-out loud-to God and the universe that her choice was to live-to face whatever she had to with courage, in order to grow her soul. She says she surrendered to a trust that, even if she didn't know how, each experience, good and bad, would contribute to her growth. This is certainly an impressive way to deal with the ups and downs of life: every one of them will somehow make you stronger, smarter, and wiser.

INTERVIEW:

K. C. Armstrong: Our next guest, Misti Rains is an educator, a mom, a spiritual guide, and an author. Her book, *Misti Moments: The Collection,* is connecting with so many readers and, I promise you, her life will inspire you. She'll discuss finding that balance between life's responsibilities: having a career, being a mom, and maintaining a healthy life and healthy relationships. You'll hear about her medical death sentence, difficult relationships and loss. But first I'd like to read a quote I found on her website.

> *I came to a place in my life where I didn't want my happiness to be based on whether or not another person was making me happy. If I had to depend on someone else, then I was placing the responsibility upon them to keep me content.*

The truth of this statement really struck me. Isn't that what we all do at some point? Isn't it hard to determine our own lives if we give away the control to others? And isn't that expectation also unfair pressure to put on someone else? We'll hear from Misti about these and other issues, but first I'd like to introduce Ms. Misti Rains. Misti, how are you today?

Misti Rains: Oh, thank you for that beautiful introduction. What you've done with the *World's Most Amazing People* is so inspiring and beautiful, and it's just a privilege to be here.

K. C. Armstrong: Thank you, Misti. From the time that we first talked, I hoped to learn more about you and help

> **My mother was my greatest love and her death my greatest sorrow. I had to rise up to focus on what was remaining, which for me was my children.**

get your story out to inspire others. Let's start out back home in Alabama, OK?

Misti Rains: OK. I grew up in the South surrounded by cotton fields, spending many lazy days on the lake. I guess I was an unusual kid; I would lay on my trampoline at night and stare at the stars. I wrote from the time I was little and am told I was incredibly philosophical and looked into things deeply, for a child. That would be a logical result of my mom's influence. She helped us see the meaning behind what seems apparent or obvious in life. She led me in helping and encouraging people without fear or embarrassment. At the National Prayer Around the Flag Pole Day, I was always the person leading the prayer and doing whatever else I could to help make a positive impact in my community. I believe that if you look back at your life, you can see traces of your destiny.

K. C. Armstrong: It sounds like your mom was a great teacher!

Misti Rains: She was. But not only by example; she was actually a high school guidance counselor, and my dad was the principal of the vocational school in my hometown. There was really no getting away with anything for me growing up!

K. C. Armstrong: That couldn't have always been easy. Were you always close to your mother?

Misti Rains: Absolutely. She was so much more than just my mom and my guidance counselor. She was my stability, my rock—my source of wisdom and strength. I watched as my mom grew throughout her life and her experiences. She was a true angel for my sister and me, always sharing with us and wanting us to rise above, to improve ourselves. She taught us virtues and spiritual depth and the ability to look beyond the superficial.

K. C. Armstrong: How long has your mother been gone?

Misti Rains: She passed away just this past year. My step dad had been sick for a long time with a seven year battle with cancer. I watched my mother dote on him all that time with the best of care. He died on Labor Day of last year, and just two months later, we received the shock of our lives when our mom followed him.

Mom was only 69 when my sister and I walked into her room to find she had died of a heart attack in her sleep. She had always seemed perfectly healthy. That discovery was the greatest devastation I have ever known. My mother was my greatest love and her death my greatest sorrow. I had to rise up to focus on what was remaining, which for me was my children. My mother instilled that piece of wisdom in us all, as though she knew we would be needing it.

K. C. Armstrong: My sincere condolences, Misti. You may have been somewhat prepared for the death of your step-father, but your mother seemed to be fine. I can't imagine how that must've been for you and your sister with absolutely no warning at all.

But there was already a lot going on in your life when this happened. If we can leave this subject for a minute, let me backtrack to your youth. What was your immediate path out of high school?

Misti Rains: After high school I went to college to become an elementary school teacher. While at college, I got involved in mission work. I was the girl that would spend spring break painting an orphanage or my summers volunteering somewhere on the other side of the world!

I always had a love for that work, and it led to meeting my husband, who was one of the original members of the band, *Mercy Me*. We married, and I spent the next fifteen years traveling with his group, which was huge in the Christian music industry. Together, my husband and I climbed the ladder of success in many ways, but ultimately that took a heavy toll on our marriage. We married young and ended up divorcing. At the time, we were each on our own healing journey which prodded us to really work through a lot of things in our relationship. That was fortunate, as we were able to remain good friends and raise three beautiful children together.

K. C. Armstrong: In my view, that's one of the most remarkable and admirable parts of your story. You guys were always there for the kids and maintained a friendship for their benefit. Very different from the horrible stories you hear about what kids of divorce often have to endure.

Misti Rains: My parents went through a messy divorce when I was a child, and it was traumatic for me. My ex and I tried to avoid that, and we both gave our children top priority. We didn't want them to be torn between two people, feeling like they had to choose a relationship with one over the other. Everybody deserves to have the freedom to love their mom and their dad without listening to accusations and complaints.

So we stayed good friends, still are, but that friendship came with a lot of work: love, forgiveness and healing. It was a process, and I did hit a serious low point where I felt I was being bombarded by emotional stress.

K. C. Armstrong: In the introduction to your chapter, I read a quote by you warning about depending on someone else to make us happy. Do you think that applied to some extent here? Do you think you were looking to your husband for your happiness—to solve the mutual stressors of a long term relationship, a demanding career and schedule, plus raising the children?

Misti Rains: Looking back, I was definitely looking for external circumstances and other people to fill a void within me. I looked to other people for fulfillment, instead of pulling from that light within my own soul. After a lengthy process, I was able to realize that fulfillment had to come from within myself. I still work on it every single day because, the truth is, we really don't need anyone to *make* us happy.

I think Jerry Maguire messed us all up, you know, making us feel like we needed another person to be complete! I came to a point where I no longer wanted to be in a relationship with someone because we made one another happy, but instead because we already knew how to be happy and thus could be together. The experience is so much more rewarding when you have two people that are not trying to extract from one another to fix things within themselves that are broken. Now, I think a healthy relationship is when both parties are confident, independent, and happy within themselves. Only then can two people come together and create something greater than the sum of its parts.

K. C. Armstrong: Eventually you remarried and ended up going through another divorce. Obviously, that relationship didn't turn out the way you had hoped it would, either. That must have been another hard hit emotionally for you.

Misti Rains: Sometimes, you know, we go through things behind closed doors and we wear a smile to the world that is really hiding a lot of pain. That was my circumstance. I lived with that pretense, on an imaginary pedestal, and the pressure of all of that just came down on me so hard.

It was a time in my life of getting on my knees and being genuine with myself about where I was in my life. What was going on around and inside me was building, like the pressure in an overinflated balloon about to explode. Whether as a result of my own doing or having been on the receiving end of so much trauma, eventually I developed a brain aneurysm.

K. C. Armstrong: Are you saying that going through stress and being in a painful relationship can actually have such an extreme physical impact on somebody?

Misti Rains: I definitely believe that. Our environment is critical to our well-being. A plant has certain requirements to thrive. Animals require certain environments to survive. You can't take animals that live in the tropics and throw them into the Arctic. Plus, there are certain things that we all need to flourish, like unconditional love and encouragement.

Negativity and criticism are health hazards. You have to keep your space guarded and sacred. Life has taught me the significance of that. It's your lifeline, you know? When that space gets contaminated, it can really knock the wind out of you. It can take a lot of people out.

K. C. Armstrong: Absolutely. That was a big turning point in your life. Here you are at a time where you're challenging your beliefs and discover you have, of all things, a brain aneurysm. You have to dig deep to find the strength to either go one way or the other. You're facing death. You talk about the power of the human spirit and believe it is present in all of us. But what helped you to get over living in a strained relationship and having a condition that should have killed you?

Misti Rains: There was this moment when I was given a death sentence. There was nothing the doctors could do for me because the aneurysm was growing in the middle of my brain stem. Removal would mean cutting through healthy brain stem tissue which would cause irreparable damage, perhaps leaving me brain dead. When you're faced with something like that, you really have to ask yourself the tough questions.

I reached out to a spiritual mentor that had been recommended to me, and he surprised me by saying, "I have one question before I'll work with you. Do you want to be here?"

My first reaction was, "Well, *of course* I want to be here! Why do you think I'm coming to you for counseling?" But his words so pierced me, tears began to fall down my face and, ultimately, it was an awakening. All those moments that I had felt trapped or that life was just too hard—I had created my own exit point mentally and emotionally. It felt like I just wanted to get out. I was praying for Jesus to come back, for all the wrong reasons.

K. C. Armstrong: But that's just where you were at that point. So much stress going on...

Misti Rains: Right. But still, I realized that I had to face a very real choice; I could choose life or choose death. I didn't *have* to be here. His question wasn't rhetorical; it required more than an automatic, knee-jerk response. I wondered if I'd created this moment in my life, and if I really just wanted to check out. I thought of Fraulein Maria in *The Sound of Music* who had to face her mountain. Did I have the courage—or the desire—to face my challenge as she did?

> *The greatest love story ever told is living inside of you, and it is your beautiful mission to create that story.*

I could try to heal and face the hard stuff by really looking at the person in the mirror instead of blaming everybody else and blaming life and blaming God. Once I did that, I recognized things within myself that I had to think differently about.

K. C. Armstrong: When your world was turned upside down, I can think of two refuges you may have found for guidance: your mother, who you've told us was so wise and loving, and your faith. Were these a comfort to you?

Misti Rains: As I mentioned, I was very, very close to my mom, and she was there for me through all of the shock, indecision and fear.

My parents thought they were losing me. Life has a way, sometimes, of catching us on the blind side and ironically, I actually lost both my parents within two months of one another just last year. It was through my experience with the aneurysm that I learned to cope with those losses.

While I was going through my health crisis, I concentrated on training my mind and my emotions. I was on a deep spiritual search and studying avidly. I worked through moments of crying out to God, asking for meaning and clarity. Finally, I learned how powerful we are on the inside. I learned that there was something much greater than me, a spirit that I could tap into to find happiness, even when I should be sad. There was a force that could pick me up when I didn't have strength. Later, when I lost my mom, I could find that spirit again.

As she taught me, you can focus on what you've lost, or you can focus on what remains. You can approach loss and despair through whatever lens you want to use. When we look at life with the filters of truth, understanding and wisdom, we can find acceptance, and that's what I was able to do. I came to a peace in my life which I truly embraced, and I accepted that everything was working together for my good. I made a decision to believe that philosophy because I didn't want to live in a world where it wasn't so.

K. C. Armstrong: You called that conscious decision "mind over matter." Are we all sent these little signs or feelings that no matter how bad it gets, there is always hope? Even so, I find it hard to imagine recognizing that truth when faced with the probability of leaving your parents and children behind at such a young age.

Misti Rains: There was an angel watching and assuring me that the universe was, you know, cheering for me. I felt there was meaning in my circumstances. I was able to seek for the value in whatever that moment was there to teach me, to surrender to a sense of trust. That was my turning point, a surrender of the soul. I think life can break you to the point where you surrender to whatever you have to face. Whether that's grief or loss or heartbreak or betrayal, we get to a point where we say, "I'm going to face this with courage and strength and trust that it's for my good." When I started approaching it that way, life became very good for me. I found peace within myself despite the circumstances in my life.

K. C. Armstrong: Wait! I have to stop you and say, "You were told that you were going to die! You remember that, right?" Misti, it's just remarkable that you could find such wisdom in that situation.

> *Today's heroes are people that overcome what's going on in their lives that others don't even know about.*

Misti Rains: Initially I had a lot, a lot of fear. One morning I woke up unable to take a breath. Each attempt was a gasp, and I lost all vision, hearing and feeling down the right side of my body. I was in a void and smashed my face as I fell to the kitchen floor. I regained consciousness in an ambulance, being rushed to the ER. All the way I repeated to myself, "I choose life."

As the team of paramedics administered morphine, I remember making this declaration to God, to the universe: "I want you to hear me; I choose to be here. I choose to go through whatever I have to face to grow my soul and to experience everything that I came here for, and I surrender to my soul's needs."

I didn't know at the time I would lose my mother or that I would go through another divorce. I didn't know all that was coming, but I made a decision in the ambulance that day that I chose to be here. I chose life. I was still breathing for a reason. I had three children, and my story wasn't over. I wasn't going to live on pain meds, and I wasn't going to allow drugs to soothe me. I was going to face life spiritually and do the hard work of inner healing. I knew that if I healed my heart and my mind, that my body would follow suit.

K. C. Armstrong: Misti, where did you get this toughness from? Is this your mother coming through you?

Misti Rains: She was surely my angel. But you know, K. C., you talk to amazing people on your program every day. For me, amazing people are most often not going to be written about in history books. They are people we meet every day, like the mom that feels discouraged and overwhelmed but gets up every morning and struggles to maintain joy in her heart.

Today's heroes are people that overcome what's going on in their lives that others don't even know about. You and I were talking earlier about how we have no idea what others are going through and how hard they may be working behind the curtains to keep an emotional stability and thrive.

We're all dealing with layers of circumstance and can never really explain them to people who are dealing with a lifetime of their own. And so I think that what makes somebody really amazing is rising up out of mental or physical challenges to shine in the realization that they can change the tide.

It's like they say, *you change your mind, you change your life* because your perspective changes. Once this happens, the whole landscape of your life is altered forever. I believe that when we heal the things within us, our outer reality will come into alignment with what's within.

K. C. Armstrong: So are you saying Misti, as a woman who was told she was going to die, that we all have that perseverance inside of us to get through whatever life throws our way?

Misti Rains: It is. My journey actually began when my first marriage crumbled. My first husband and I had risen to the height of success, from the world's perspective, but my life fell apart anyway. It was a pivotal moment for me. That was when life first humbled me, but we're never intended to stay in that place of discouragement. At that low point, feeling that my world had unraveled, I began to feel God's love.

It's hard to let go of the dream of 2.5 kids, a Labrador retriever and a seat on the Sunday school committee. But once I recognized that stereotype for what it is, I began to feel God's love in a way that I had never known. That freedom allowed me to truly feel an embrace by the entire universe, to feel loved unconditionally and even protected, if that makes sense.

Through the disintegration of my marriage and then my tragic health experience, I felt like I had lost everything, but I had also found everything. A new kind of love began to heal me and created a thirst for more of that. I grew my relationship with that voice inside my soul, and it took me on a journey of healing. The life and death situation, the loss of someone who was the greatest love of my life, my divorce—it all was very valuable for the journey that God has taken me on, and I've needed all of it.

K. C. Armstrong: To be able to welcome such pain as necessary for spiritual growth is too much to believe. That has to be the height of acceptance, perhaps wisdom.

Misti Rains: K.C., there was a time when I didn't think I could ever be happy. I didn't think it was in the cards for me. I thought my life was over or at least so messed up that it could never be fixed. Have you ever felt like that?

K. C. Armstrong: I'm sure everybody out there has lost hope at some point. I have a gremlin who sits on my shoulder, and I call him the

Turk. He's the one that tells me that I can't, and I'm always out to beat the Turk.

Misti Rains: Right. We all know him. But when you really want to heal, you have to consider the connection between your emotions and your body. Honestly, as weird as that sounds, I think we have more power than many think to heal through that connection. We're stronger and more resilient than we could ever imagine ourselves to be.

You know, a lot of people die instantly from an aneurysm like I had. I was so fortunate. I spent a full year learning to use my hand again, re-learning how to walk up stairs. There was a time I didn't know if I would ever write or speak again. Was it coincidence that my afflictions affected my main means of validation in my life? My hand and my mouth had both become numb, preventing me from living my passion and doing what I felt I was put on this earth to do—speaking and writing.

I believe my body was tired of performing. During that time I believe God was trying to teach me something. I was using my gifts wrongly. I was using them as a means to prove my worth and to feel validated, significant, and loved. I had to learn to truly love myself and accept that I was already worthy, valuable, and loved simply because of the intrinsic worth God has placed within me, and that God has placed within us all.

I seemed to feel the universe telling me, "Healer, heal thyself." I created a chapter in my book called *Dear Body, Please Forgive Me* which includes my apologies to myself as part of my healing. I wanted forgiveness for the way I sometimes treated myself and talked to myself. We all can fall into that negative chatter, you know? As I worked on those things, I went in for an M.R.I. This time the deadly aneurysm looked more like a benign brain tumor. It was shrinking. The neurosurgeons were speechless and without a medical explanation. But

I knew what was happening: I was healing my mind, and that was healing my body.

K. C. Armstrong: Misti, I have to tell you, you nailed it. I can say with all conviction that you are one of the world's most amazing people. Even by your own standards; you said earlier, "what makes somebody really amazing is rising up out of mental or physical challenges to shine in the realization that they can change the tide." You have risen from loss, disappointment and the threat of an early death. But in all this, you found acceptance, and even meaning. I don't know how you were able to do that.

What would you specifically like to tell anyone who might be in a position like yours? How do they find hope and courage?

Misti Rains: The biggest thing is for them to know that they already have all the support that they need. There is a higher power and you can pull from that strength. When we cry out, help comes in many ways. If they're holding anger, jealousy, hurt, or resentment, anything not in alignment with love and peace, they must address that to heal their heart. One of the greatest truths is that we are not a victim to our circumstances, and we don't have to be defined by anyone else. The greatest love story ever told is living inside of you, and it is your beautiful mission to create that story. Whatever comes your way is meant for you, and you can use it to learn and grow.

K. C. Armstrong: Misti, I love your positive attitude and the way you actually welcomed the adversities into your life as teaching tools. The introspection and analysis required reminds me of one of your very first comments, about being a child who really analyzed things. You attributed that to your mother's influence, and we can see that she really was an angel rooting for you your whole life.

Misti Rains: Yes, KC, thanks for that insight. Those nights on the hammock studying the sky probably helped me find the patience to be still long enough to see how my struggles could actually benefit my life. That stillness is important. So many of us rush around without being involved in what's around us.

K. C. Armstrong: I can't argue with that! Between the phones, technology, and the daily routine, it's easy to allow one day to just slide into the next.

Misti Rains: Absolutely. My advice would be to appreciate each individual moment. Put your phone down. Look around and be present when you're standing in line at the supermarket. Slow down and look the cashier in the eyes. This may be the last day you have with your health, your family, your loved ones. Not to be pessimistic, but at the time, I didn't know I was celebrating the last holiday I would ever experience with my family and that everything was about to end so abruptly for us; but it did. I would just say be aware and be grateful. Listen to what life is saying to you because it's speaking magically all the time, guiding you and helping you along your way. Listen. Be present.

K. C. Armstrong: Well said, Misti. Thank you for sharing your words and your truly amazing story. And thank you for a great example of what it means to be one of the *World's Most Amazing Women.*

More information about Misti:

Website: www.mistirains.com
Book: *Misti Moments: The Collection*

ACKNOWLEDGEMENTS

My heartfelt thanks to all the brave women interviewed within this book that have opened their lives to show us ways that have helped them find peace and happiness. It's remarkable to me to see the common themes in these very different struggles: faith, forgiveness, acceptance, perseverance, compassion and self acceptance. Each story suggests that pain can be used productively to grow our understanding of the world, perhaps our spirituality. I look at this series as a beacon, shining light on paths that have worked for others and, hopefully, will add new possibilities for readers to consider.

Kathy Bidelman
Cicilia Seleyian
Debra Morgan
R. Jade McAuliffe
Danielle Shay
Marilynn Hughes
Marcy Stone
Sandi Holst
Dr. Feyi Obamehinti
Lola Scarborough
Wendy Ann
Lotus Prana Zheng
Misti Rains

BOOK CLUB QUESTIONS

FOR DISCUSSION:

1. What is the impact of the author's voice heard throughout the book?
2. With which interviewee do you most closely relate, and why?
3. List three things you learned (fact or insight) referencing chapter numbers and titles.
4. Are there any situations that you would have handled much differently? Discuss your different approach and why you would have taken those actions.
5. If you prepared a survey for most inspiring chapter, which 4 chapters would you include in your list of choices?
6. Did any of the chapters raise topics or questions you would like to research?
7. If you could ask one question of any of the authors, what would it be, and to whom?
8. Which of these people would you most like to invite for dinner? What would you serve, and to what topic would you lead the conversation?

Responses to these questions or general comments may be submitted to www.wmapradio.com. Selected submissions will be posted for online or on-air discussion.

Like this book? One of the best ways to thank an author is to post a review on Amazon, Barnes and Noble, Goodreads, your blog or social media.

9 781734 705805